The
LEARN to
KNIT a SWEATER
BOOK

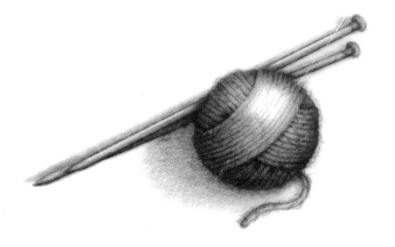

Bobbie Matela, Managing Editor
Carol Wilson Mansfield, Art Director
Mary Ann Frits, Editorial Director
Kelly Robinson, Sandy Scoville, Kathy Wesley, Editorial Staff
Graphic Solutions inc-chgo, Book Design

For a full-color catalog including
books of knit and crochet designs,
write to:

American School of Needlework®
Consumer Division
1455 Linda Vista Drive
San Marcos, CA 92069

Shown on front cover: *World's Easiest Cardigan* and *Challenge Sweater*.

Patterns tested and models made by Mary Ann Frits, Bobbie Matela, Dolores Roberts, Kelly Robinson, Sandy Scoville, Rita Weiss, and Kathy Wesley.

©1998 by American School of Needlework®, Inc.; ASN Publishing, 1455 Linda Vista Drive, San Marcos, CA 92069
ISBN: 0-88195-850-6   All rights reserved.   Printed in U.S.A.

Introduction

Sweaters, sweaters, everywhere! Sweaters have become one of today's hottest fashions, designed with a new fit that's comfortable, loose, and easy to wear.

And if you've always wanted to knit your own sweater, this book is for you. Whatever your size and shape, you can welcome these sweaters to your wardrobe—we've even included Plus Sizes in the instructions.

With our easy, step-by-step picture method you can learn all the basics of knitting in just a few hours—and you can do it all by yourself with no one to help you! Our lessons are easy to follow, with no difficult stitches, no complicated instructions. In fact, we've even written our patterns without the traditional abbreviations that often confuse beginners. It's like we're sitting right there beside you giving you special hints and helps along the way.

And once you've mastered the basics, you can go right on to make one of our wonderful sweaters. They're designed by Lion Brand® not only to look great, but to be knitted by a beginner.

We'd love to see pictures of the sweaters you make from this book. Send a picture we can keep to:

> Yes I Knitted A Sweater!
> c/o ASN Publishing
> 1455 Linda Vista Drive
> San Marcos, CA 92069

Have fun and wear your new sweater with pride—now let's go shopping.

Jean Leinhauser
President

About the yarns...

We've chosen to knit our sweaters in a variety of interesting types and exciting colors of Lion Brand® yarns. Famous for quality since 1878, Lion Brand® is known for its high standard of quality, unique texture and beautiful color combinations. If you wish to use other brands, just be sure to substitute the same yarn weight, and check for gauge and yardages on the skein.

If you can't find these beautiful Lion Brand® yarns at your favorite store, contact Lion Brand® at 1-800-258-YARN.

A word to the left-handed...

Knitting is a two-handed process in which both hands are used almost equally. So left-handers do not need to worry about learning a different method. Knitting may seem awkward at first, but this is true for all beginning knitters.

Getting Started

To knit, you need only a pair of knitting needles, some yarn, a tape measure, a crochet hook and a pair of scissors. Later on, you can add all kinds of accessories, from needle point protectors to stitch holders to cable needles to a tapestry needle. But for now, the supplies listed above are all you really need.

Yarn

Yarn comes in a wonderful selection of materials, textures, sizes and colors, ranging from wool to metallic, lumpy to smooth, gossamer fine to chunky, and from the palest pastels to vibrant neon shades.

The most commonly used yarn, and the one you'll need for the lessons in this book, is worsted weight (sometimes called 4-ply). It is readily available in a wide variety of beautiful colors. Choose a light color for practice — it will be much easier to see the individual stitches.

Always read yarn labels carefully. The label will tell you how much yarn is in the skein or ball, in ounces, grams or yards; the type of yarn, how to care for it, and sometimes how to pull the yarn from the skein (and yes, there is a trick to this!). The label usually bears a dye lot number, which assures you that the color of each skein with this same number is identical. The same color may vary from dye lot to dye lot, creating unsightly variations in color when a project is finished. So when purchasing yarn for a sweater, be sure to match the dye lot number on the skeins.

You'll need a blunt-pointed steel tapestry sewing needle with an eye big enough to carry the yarn for weaving in ends and joining pieces, or you can buy big plastic sewing needles called yarn needles.

Crochet Hooks

Even though you're knitting, not crocheting, you'll need to have an aluminum crochet hook handy for correcting mistakes, retrieving dropped stitches, and for some finishing techniques. You don't need to know how to crochet, though!

The size hook you need depends on the thickness of the yarn you are using and the size of the knitting needles.

Here's a handy chart to show you what size hook to use:

Knitting Needle Size	Crochet Hook Size
7-8-9	G
10 and 10 1/2	H
11 and 13	I
15 and 17	J

Knitting Needles

Knitting needles come in pairs of straight needles with a shaped point at one end and a knob at the other end of each needle so that the stitches won't slide off; in sets of four or five double-pointed needles used for making seamless small projects; and in circular form with a point at each end.

You will most often use straight needles, which are readily available in both aluminum and bamboo. Both materials are equally good. The straight needles come in two lengths: 10 inches and 14 inches. For our lessons, we will use the 10-inch length.

The needles also come in a variety of sizes, which refer to the diameter and thus the size of the stitch you can make with them. These are numbered from 0 (the smallest usually available) to 17 (the largest usually available). For our lessons, we use a size 8 needle, an average size for use with worsted weight yarn.

Let's look at a knitting needle:

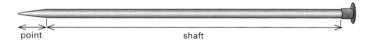

Now with your yarn and needles ready, let's get started.

Lesson 1

Casting On

Knitting always starts with a row of foundation stitches worked onto one needle. Making a foundation row is called casting on. Although there are several ways of casting on, the one which follows is easiest for beginners.

Step 1:

Make a slip knot on one needle as follows: Make a yarn loop, leaving about 6" length of yarn at free end.

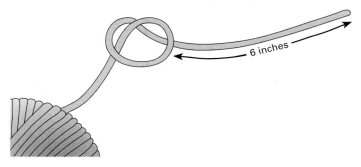

Insert knitting needle into loop and draw up yarn from free end to make a loop on needle.

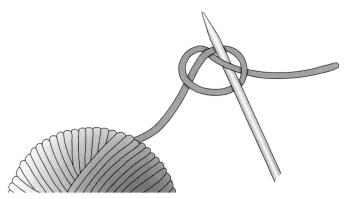

Pull yarn firmly, but not tightly, to form a slip knot on the shaft, not the point, of the needle. Pull yarn end to tighten the loop. This slip knot counts as your first stitch.

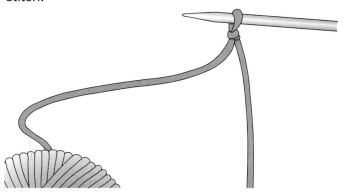

Step 2:

Hold the needle with the knot in your left hand, placing the thumb and index finger close to the point of the needle, which helps you control it.

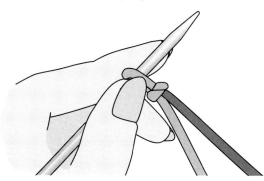

Step 3:

Your right hand will control the yarn coming from the skein; to help keep your tension even, hold the yarn loosely against the palm of your hand with three fingers, and then up and over your index finger.
A and **B** show how this looks from above the hand and beneath the hand.

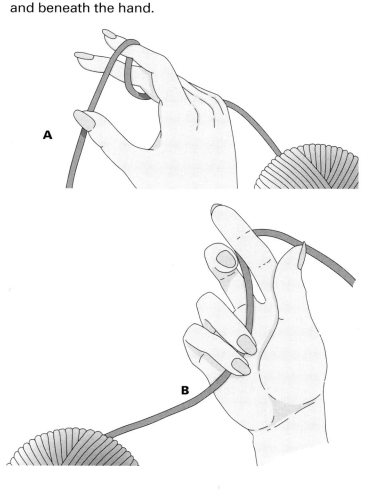

Step 4:

Hold the other needle with your right hand, again with your fingers close to the point. Grasp the needle firmly, but not tightly.

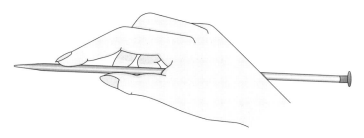

Step 5:

Insert the point of the right needle - from front to back - into the slip knot and under the left needle.

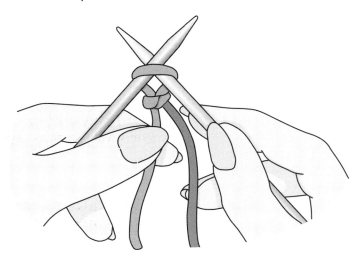

Step 6:

Continuing to hold left needle in your left hand, move left fingers over to brace right needle.

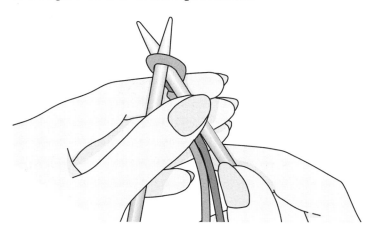

With right index finger, pick up the yarn from the skein and,

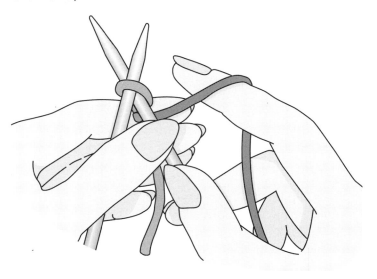

releasing right hand's grip on the right needle, bring yarn under and over the point of right needle.

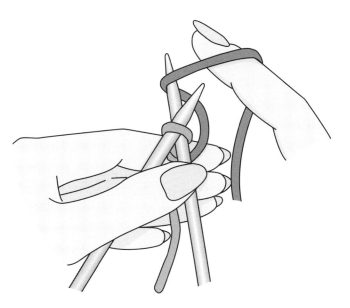

Step 7:

Returning right fingers to right needle, draw yarn through stitch with point of right needle.

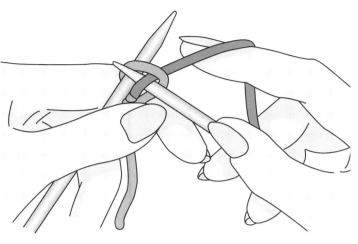

Step 8:

Slide left needle point into new stitch.

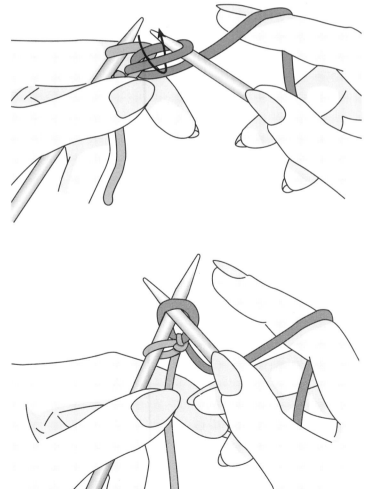

Step 9:

Remove right needle; then pull skein yarn gently, but **not** tightly, to make stitch snug on needle; you should be able to slip the stitch back and forth on the shaft of the needle easily.

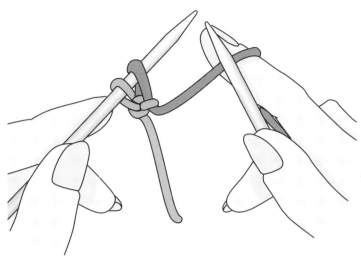

You have now made one stitch, and there are two stitches on left needle (remember the slip knot always counts as a stitch).

Step 10:

Insert point of right needle - from front to back - into stitch you've just made and under left needle.

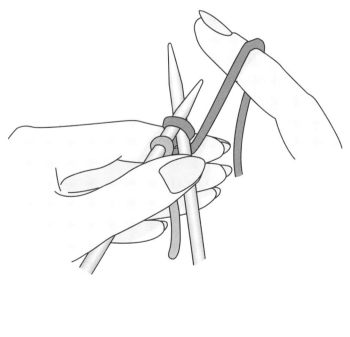

Repeat Steps 6 through 10 for next stitch. Continue repeating Steps 6 through 10 until you have 24 stitches on the left needle. Be sure to pull each new stitch up, off the point and onto the shaft of the left needle.

Now stop, relax, get a cup of coffee or a soda, and look at your work. It's probably tight and uneven, which is normal for a beginner. As you practice and begin to feel less clumsy, your work will automatically become more even.

Now after all that work, guess what you're going to do next — destroy it! To do this, pull the needle out from the stitches, then wind the used yarn back on the skein or ball. Begin again and cast on 24 stitches, trying this time to work more evenly, keeping each stitch snug but not tight.

Hint: Beginners usually knit very tightly, making it hard to slide the stitches on the needle. Try to relax; it is better to work too loosely in the begining, than too tightly. Take care not to make your stitches on the point of the needle; instead, slide the needle shaft well through each stitch as you work. Always be sure to insert needle under full thickness of yarn, to avoid "splitting" the yarn.

Lesson 2

The Knit Stitch

All knitting is made up of only two basic stitches, the knit stitch and the purl stitch. These are combined in many ways to create different effects and textures. And guess what—now you're half way to being a knitter—for you've already learned the knit stitch as you practiced casting on! That's because the first three steps of the knit stitch are exactly like casting on.

Step 1:

Hold the needle with the 24 cast-on stitches from Lesson 1 in your left hand. Insert point of right needle in first stitch, from front to back under the left needle, just as in casting on.

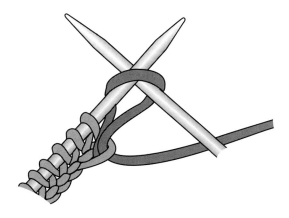

Step 2:

With right index finger, bring yarn from skein under and over point of right needle.

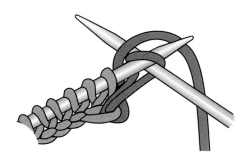

Step 3:

Draw yarn through stitch with right needle point.

Step 4:

The next step now differs from casting on. Slip the first loop on the left needle off, so the new stitch is entirely on the right needle.

Now you've completed your first knit stitch! Repeat these four steps in each stitch remaining on the left needle. When all stitches are on the right needle and the left needle is free, one row has been completed. Turn right needle, hold it now in your left hand and take free needle in your right hand. Work another row of stitches in same manner as last row, taking care not to work tightly.

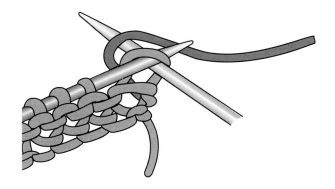

Work 10 more rows of knit stitches.

The pattern formed by knitting every row is called garter stitch (we don't really know why!), and looks the same on both sides. When counting rows in **garter stitch**, each raised ridge (a ridge is indicated by the box in the photo below) indicates you have knitted two rows.

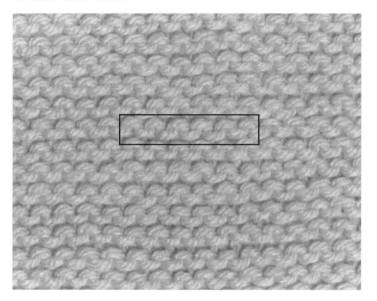

Break time!

Lesson 3

The Purl Stitch

The reverse of the knit stitch is called the purl stitch. Instead of inserting the right needle point from left to right under the left needle (as you did for the knit stitch), you will now insert it from right to left, in front of the left needle. Work as follows on the 24 stitches already on your needle.

Step 1:

Insert right needle, from right to left, into first stitch, and in front of left needle.

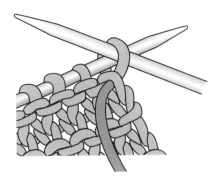

Step 2:

Holding yarn in front of work (side toward you), bring it around right needle counterclockwise.

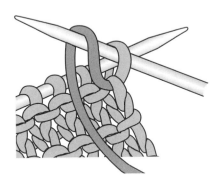

Step 3:

With right needle, pull yarn back through stitch.

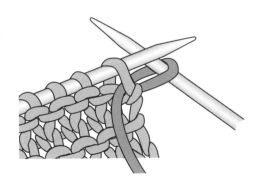

Slide stitch off left needle, leaving new stitch on right needle.

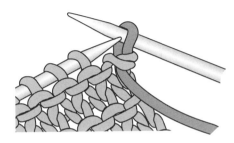

Your first purl stitch is now completed. Continue to repeat these three steps in every stitch across the row. The row you have just purled will be considered the wrong side of your work at the moment.

Now transfer the needle with stitches from right to left hand; the side of the work now facing you is called the right side of your work. Knit every stitch in the row; at end of row, transfer needle with stitches to left hand, then purl every stitch in the row. Knit across another row, purl across another row.

Now stop and look at your work; by alternating knit and purl rows, you are creating one of the most frequently used stitch patterns in knitting, **stockinette stitch**.

Turn the work over to the knit side; it should look like stitches in the photo on the left. The purl side of the work should look like stitches in the photo on the right.

knit side

purl side

Continue with your practice piece, alternately knitting and purling rows, until you feel comfortable with the needles and yarn. As you work you'll see that your piece will begin to look more even.

Hold your hands in a comfortable relaxed position near your lap. The more comfortable you are, the more even your work will be.

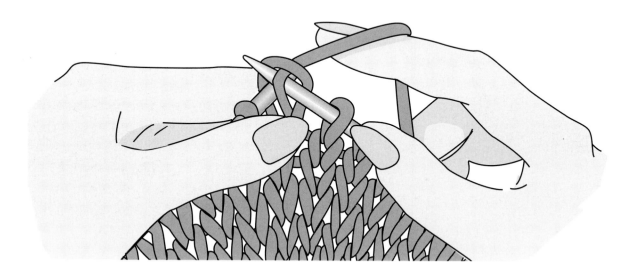

Lesson 4

Correcting Mistakes

Dropped Stitches

Each time you knit or purl a stitch, take care to pull the stitch off the left needle after completing the new stitch. Otherwise, you will be adding stitches when you don't want to. But if you let a stitch slip off the needle **before** you've knitted or purled it - that's called a dropped stitch. Even expert knitters drop a stitch now and then, but a dropped stitch must be picked up and put back on the needle. If not, the stitch will "run" down the length of the piece just like a run in a stocking!

If you notice the dropped stitch right away, and it has not run down more than one row, you can usually easily place it back on the needle.

But if it has dropped several rows, you'll find it easier to use a crochet hook to work the stitch back up to the needle. Here's how.

On the knit side (right side of work) of the stockinette stitch, insert the crochet hook into the dropped stitch from front to back, under the horizontal strand in the row above.

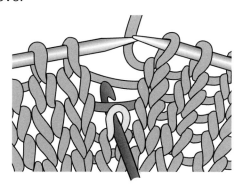

Hook the horizontal strand above and pull through the loop on the crochet hook. Continue in this manner until you reach the last row worked, then transfer the loop from the crochet hook to the left needle, being careful not to twist it.

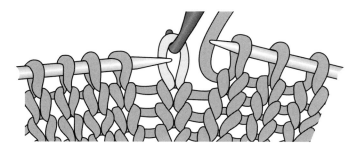

To pick up knit stitches in any other pattern stitch, you will insert the crochet hook into the dropped stitch from the front to the back, under the horizontal strand in the row above. For the purled stitches, you will move the horizontal strand in front of the dropped stitch and insert the crochet hook into the dropped stitch from the back to the front, over the horizontal strand. Hook the horizontal strand and pull through the loop on the crochet hook.

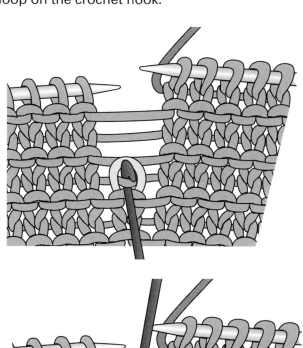

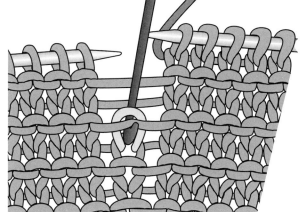

Unraveling Stitches

Sometimes it is necessary to unravel a large number of stitches, even down several rows, to correct a mistake. Whenever possible, carefully unravel the stitches one-by-one by putting the needle into the row below and undoing the stitch above, until the mistake is reached.

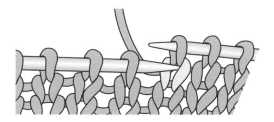

If several rows need to be unraveled, carefully slide all stitches off the needle and unravel each row down to the row in which the error occurred. Then unravel this row, stitch by stitch, placing each stitch back on the needle in the correct position, without twisting it.

Joining Yarn

New yarn should be added only at the beginning of a row, never in the middle of a row, unless this is required for a color pattern change. To add yarn, tie the new strand around the old strand, making a knot at the edge of work, leaving at least a 6" end on both old and new strands. Then proceed to knit with the new yarn. The ends will be hidden later by weaving in.

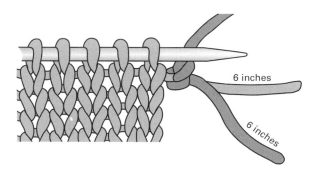

6 inches

6 inches

Lesson 5

Binding Off

Now you've learned how to cast on, and to knit and purl the stitches; next you need to know how to take the stitches off the needle once you've finished a piece.

The process used to secure the stitches is called binding off. Let's bind off your practice piece; be careful to work loosely for this procedure, and begin with the right side (the knit side) of your work facing you.

Knit Bind-Off

Step 1:

Knit the first 2 stitches. Now insert left needle into the first of the 2 stitches, the one you knitted first,

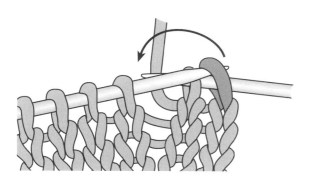

and pull it over the second stitch and completely off the needle. You have now bound off one stitch.

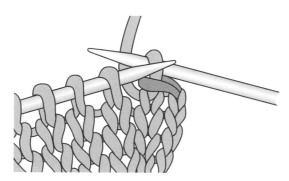

Step 2:

Knit one more stitch; insert left needle into first stitch on right needle and pull first stitch over the new stitch and completely off the needle. Another stitch is now bound off.

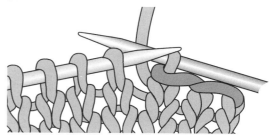

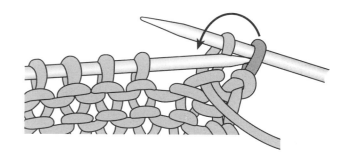

Repeat Step 2 four times more; now knit each of the 17 stitches remaining on the left needle. You have bound off 6 stitches on the knit side of your work.

To bind off on the purl side, turn your practice piece so the wrong side of your work is facing you.

Purl Bind-Off

Step 1:

Purl the first 2 stitches. Now insert left needle into the first stitch on right needle,

and pull it over the second stitch and completely off the needle. You have now bound off one stitch.

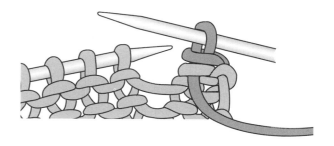

Step 2:

Purl one more stitch; insert left needle into first stitch on right needle and pull first stitch over the new stitch and completely off the needle. Another stitch is bound off.

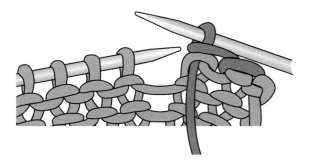

Repeat Step 2 four times more; now purl each of the 11 stitches remaining on the left needle.

Turn your work so that the right side is facing you; bind off 6 sts in the same manner that you bound off the first 6 stitches on this side, then knit remaining stitches.

Turn your work and bind off the remaining stitches on the wrong side; there will be one stitch left on the needle and you are ready to "finish off" or "end off" the yarn. To do this, cut yarn leaving about a 6" end. With needle, draw this end up through the final stitch to secure it.

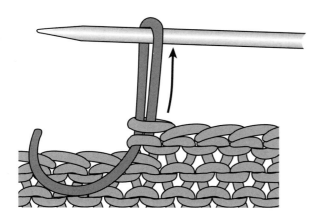

You have just learned to bind off knit stitches on the right side of your work and bind off purl stitches on the wrong side of your work. When you wish to bind off in a pattern stitch, where some stitches in a row have been knitted and others purled, knit the knit stitches and purl the purl stitches as you work across the row.

Lesson 10

The Secrets of Finishing

Maybe you've heard that the hardest part of creating a knitted garment is the finishing. This is not true if you know the secrets of finishing. To finish a knitted garment requires no special skill. However, it does require time, attention, and a knowledge of basic techniques which we describe in this section. By carefully following these finishing instructions, your well-knitted pieces will become a beautiful hand-knitted garment of which you can proudly say,

"I knit it myself."

Sewing Seams

Your pattern will usually tell you in what order to assemble the pieces. Use a tapestry sewing needle and the same yarn as used in the garment to sew the seams, unless the yarn is too thick, in which case use a thinner yarn in a matching color. Pin seams before sewing, carefully matching stitches and rows as much as possible.

Invisible Seam: This seam gives a smooth and neat appearance, as it weaves the edges together invisibly from the right side.

To join horizontal edges, such as shoulder seams, weave the edges together as shown.

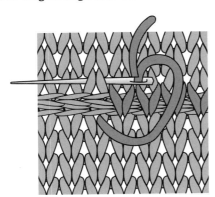

To join a front/back vertical edge to a horizontal sleeve edge, weave the edges together as shown.

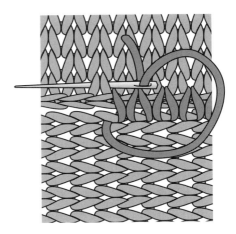

To join vertical edges, such as side seams or under-arm sleeve seams, sew the edges together on the right side as shown, pulling yarn gently until edges meet.

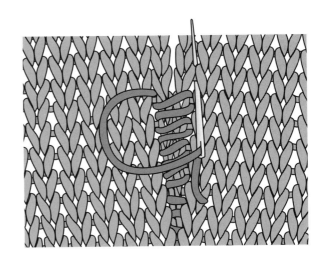

Overcast Seam: On some types of seams, an overcast stitch may be used.

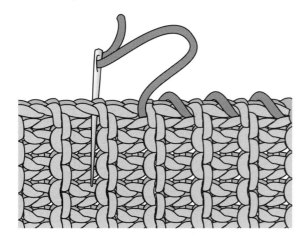

Weaving in Ends

After sewing the seams, weave in all the yarn ends securely. To do this with yarn ends at the edges of the piece, use a size 13 tapestry needle (or size indicated in the pattern) and weave the yarn ends into the seams on the wrong side as shown, weaving about 2" in one direction and then 1" in the reverse direction. Cut off excess yarn.

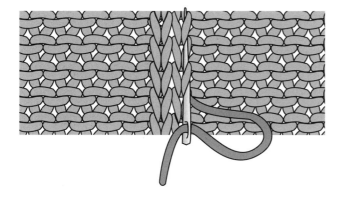

For any yarn ends that are not near seams, use a tapestry needle and weave the yarn through the backs of stitches, first weaving about 2" in one direction and then 1" in the reverse direction.
Cut off excess yarn.

Note: Never weave in more than one yarn end at a time.

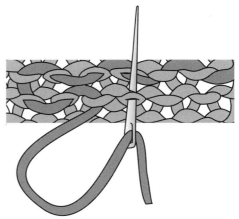

Hint: When seaming, do not draw the stitches too tightly, as the joining should have the same stretch or give as in the knitted garment.

Equipment Page

Here are the tools you'll need as you become a well-equipped knitter of sweaters.

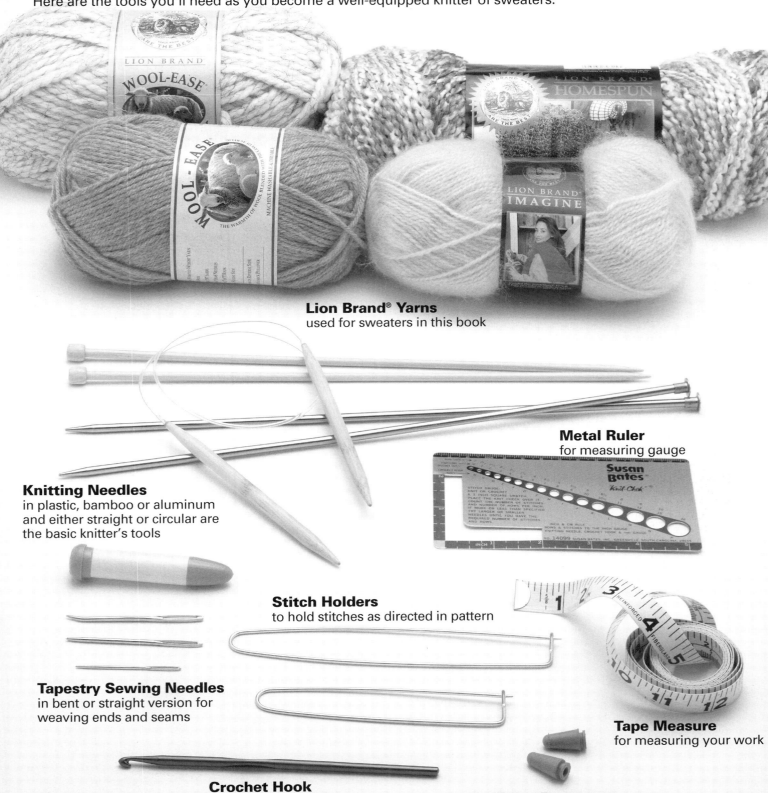

Lion Brand® Yarns
used for sweaters in this book

Knitting Needles
in plastic, bamboo or aluminum
and either straight or circular are
the basic knitter's tools

Metal Ruler
for measuring gauge

Stitch Holders
to hold stitches as directed in pattern

Tapestry Sewing Needles
in bent or straight version for
weaving ends and seams

Tape Measure
for measuring your work

Crochet Hook
for picking up stitches

Point Protectors
to keep stitches on needle
between work sessions

Which Sweater Should You Knit First?

With the exception of our "Challenge Sweater", all of the designs are easy enough for a beginner to knit. We suggest you knit at least one other sweater before trying the "Challenge Sweater."

After you've chosen the style you want to knit, the next important aspect is how it will fit. We've included a size range for each sweater that goes to a plus size 3X. Our sweaters are all designed with a loose, easy fit. To help you choose which size to make, we've included finished garment measurements with each pattern.

If you have a favorite sweater that fits you just right, measure it and then choose the pattern size that is closest to those measurements.

And the most important step for a sweater that fits perfectly — gauge, of course! Be sure to make the specified gauge swatch and change needle sizes if needed to achieve the gauge.

Design Directory

On the next four pages and the back cover, these six sweaters are shown in full-color photographs. Sweaters are shown in more than one color to help you visualize your own choice of yarn color.

This soft, cozy cardigan, worked entirely in Garter Stitch, has pockets that are formed by folding the front pieces up!

This wonderful warm sweater has a loose, easy fit with a fashionable, rolled collar!

Knitting this sweater goes so quickly, before you know it you'll be depending on it to warm you.

This three-color striped sweater is fun to knit and great to wear!

This casual wear-over-everything, V-neck sweater is toasty warm and quick to knit!

Combine four different yarns in six wonderful colors for a smashing sweater that's a challenge to knit!

PERFECT PULLOVER, knit with Wool-Ease® Thick & Quick in Pine and assembled on the pebbled side

PERFECT PULLOVER, knit with Wool-Ease® Thick & Quick in Wheat and assembled on the ribbed side

CHALLENGE SWEATER, knit in coordinating shades of Jiffy®, Homespun®, Chenille Sensations and Imagine

21

WORLD'S EASIEST CARDIGAN,
knit in Homespun® Modern blues (left),
Shaker neutrals (right) and Tudor pastels (below)

HUG ME SWEATER,
**knit with Imagine in
Blue Heather and
assembled on the
purl side**

HUG ME SWEATER,
**knit with Imagine
Autumn Leaves and
assembled on the
knit side**

HUG ME SWEATER,
**knit with Imagine Maize
and assembled on the
purl side**

2

STRIPE IT RICH SWEATER,
knit with Wool-Ease® worsted
weight yarn in Green Heather,
Chestnut Heather and
Fisherman (upper)
and in Green Heather, Rose
Heather and Fisherman (lower)

28

World's Easiest Cardigan

This soft, cozy cardigan is made in a wonderful yarn by Lion Brand called Homespun®. A thick strand of soft acrylic yarn is twisted with a thin strand of polyester for a unique textured look. The yarn, considered a bulky weight, comes in many beautiful shaded combinations, as well as coordinating solid colors. The cardigan is worked entirely in Garter Stitch (every row is knitted) in just five pieces! The front pieces are knit 8" longer than the back and then folded up, to cleverly form pockets.

Shown in color photographs on front cover and on page 26.

Sizing:

The cardigan has an easy, comfortable fit, with 8" to 10" allowed for ease. It is designed to be worn open at the front. The belt is optional.

Note: Pattern is written for size small with changes for other sizes in parentheses.

Size	Body Measurement at Bust	Finished Garment Measurement at Bust
Small	30"-32"	40"
Medium	34"-36"	44"
Large	38"-40"	48"
1X	42"-44"	52"
2X	46"-48"	56"
3X	50"-52"	60"

All measurements are approximate.

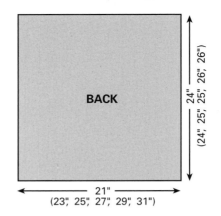

BACK

24"
(24", 25", 25", 26", 26")

21"
(23", 25", 27", 29", 31")

Materials:

Lion Brand Homespun® bulky weight yarn in 6-oz pull skeins in color of your choice (we used Tudor, Color 315; Modern, Color 304; and Shaker, Color 301 for our models)

6 skeins for size Small
7 skeins for size Medium
8 skeins for size Large
9 skeins for size 1X
10 skeins for size 2X
12 skeins for size 3X

Equipment:

Size 10, 14" straight knitting needles, or size required for gauge.
Size H aluminum crochet hook (for correcting mistakes and picking up stitches)
Size 13 steel tapestry sewing needle, or plastic yarn needle
Straight pins

Gauge:

In Garter Stitch (knit every row), 11 stitches = 4"

Making the Gauge Swatch:

To be sure the cardigan will be the correct size, begin by making a sample swatch that will let you measure your gauge.

Cast on 30 stitches. Knit 12 rows. Then loosely bind off all stitches as to knit. Place gauge swatch on a flat surface and measure in center of swatch to see if stitches are worked to gauge. There should be 11 stitches in every four inches (see **photo**). If you do not have 11 stitches in every four inches, see Lesson 8 on page 19.

Be sure your gauge is correct before you start your sweater.

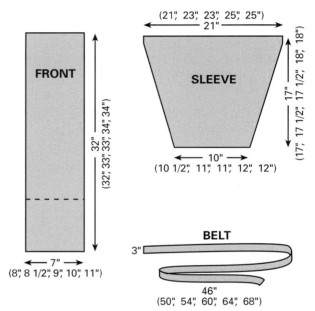

FRONT

32"
(32", 33", 33", 34", 34")

7"
(8", 8 1/2", 9", 10", 11")

(21", 23", 23", 25", 25")
21"

SLEEVE

17"
(17", 17 1/2", 17 1/2", 18", 18")

10"
(10 1/2", 11", 11", 12", 12")

BELT

3"

46"
(50", 54", 60", 64", 68")

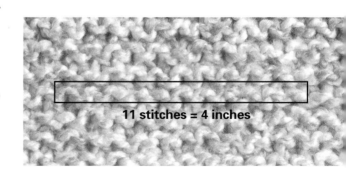

11 stitches = 4 inches

Cardigan Instructions

Note: Pattern is written for size small with changes for other sizes in parentheses.

Back

Leaving a 6" or longer yarn end, cast on 57 **(63, 68, 74, 79, 85)** stitches. Make a firm knot near the end of the 6" length of unused yarn so it won't unravel.

Row 1 (right side of garment):
Knit each stitch.

> **Hint:** Because Garter Stitch looks the same on both sides, it helps to mark the first row of each piece with contrasting yarn to identify which side is the right side.

Repeat Row 1 until piece measures 24" **(24", 25", 25", 26", 26")** from cast-on edge **(Fig 1)**.

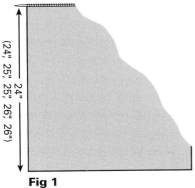

Fig 1

Loosely bind off all stitches as to knit **(Figs 2** and **3)**.

Cut yarn, leaving a 6" or longer end; knot end. Set piece aside.

Front (make 2)

Leaving a 6" or longer yarn end, cast on 20 **(23, 24, 26, 28, 30)** stitches. Knot yarn end.

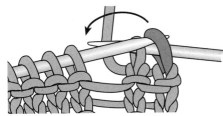

Fig 2

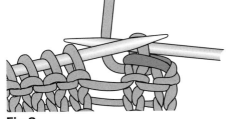

Fig 3

Row 1 (right side of garment**):**
Knit each stitch.

Repeat Row 1 until piece measure 32" (32", 33", 33", 34", 34") from cast-on edge **(Fig 4)**.

Note: Fronts are made longer than Back so that the additional 8" can be turned up for pockets.

Loosely bind off all stitches as to knit.

Cut yarn, leaving a 6" or longer yarn end; knot end. Set piece aside.

Sleeve (make 2)
Leaving a 6" or longer yarn end, cast on 27 (29, 31, 31, 33, 33) stitches. Knot yarn end.

Row 1 (right side of garment**):**
Knit each stitch.

Rows 2 and 3:
Repeat Row 1.

On the next row you will begin making increases to make the sleeve wider for the upper arm.

Row 4:
Knit first stitch, increase by knitting in front and back of next stitch **(Figs 5** and **6)**; knit to last two stitches; increase by knitting in front and back of next stitch; knit last stitch.

You should now have 29 (31, 33, 33, 35, 35) stitches.

Now you will work the next few rows differently depending on the size garment you are making. You will be increasing on every 4th row for a certain number of times, and then you will be increasing on every 6th row for a certain number of times.

For size small only:

Repeat Rows 1 through 4 three times more.

You should now have 35 stitches. Continue with "For All Sizes" on page 33.

For size medium only:

Repeat Rows 1 through 4 once more.

You should now have 33 stitches. Continue with "For All Sizes" on page 33.

For sizes large and 1X only:

Repeat Rows 1 through 4 six times more.

You should now have 45 stitches. Continue with "For All Sizes" on page 33.

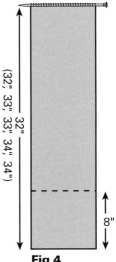

Fig 4

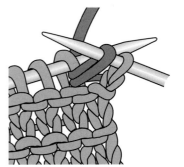

Fig 5

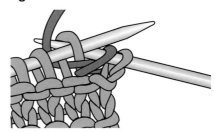

Fig 6

For sizes 2X and 3X only:

Repeat Rows 1 through 4 ten times more.

You should now have 55 stitches. Continue with "For All Sizes" below.

For All Sizes:

Now you will be increasing every 6th row.

Row 1:
Knit each stitch.

Rows 2 through 5:
Repeat Row 1.

Row 6:
Knit first stitch, increase in next stitch; knit to last two stitches; increase in next stitch; knit last stitch.

For size small only:

Repeat Rows 1 through 6 ten times more.

You should now have 57 stitches. Continue with "For All Sizes" below.

For size medium only:

Repeat Rows 1 through 6 eleven times more.

You should now have 57 stitches. Continue with "For All Sizes" below.

For sizes large and 1X only:

Repeat Rows 1 through 6 eight times more.

You should now have 63 stitches. Continue with "For All Sizes" below.

For sizes 2X and 3X only:

Repeat Rows 1 through 6 six times more.

You should now have 69 stitches. Continue with "For All Sizes" below.

For All Sizes:

Work even (knit every row with no more increases) on 57 (57, 63, 63, 69, 69) stitches until sleeve measures 17" (17", 17½", 17½", 18", 18") from cast-on edge (**Fig 7**).

Loosely bind off all stitches as to knit.

Cut yarn, leaving a 6" or longer yarn end; knot end. Set piece aside.

Belt

Leaving a 6" or longer yarn end, cast on 7 stitches. Knot yarn end.

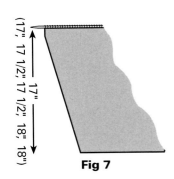

17" (17", 17½", 17½", 18", 18")

Fig 7

Row 1:

Knit each stitch.

Repeat Row 1 until piece measures 46" (50", 54", 60", 64", 68") from cast-on edge, or desired length.

Loosely bind off all stitches as to knit.

Cut yarn, leaving a 6" or longer yarn end; knot end. Set piece aside.

Finishing

Note: Refer to Lesson 10 on page 21 for information on sewing seams and weaving in ends.

Before sewing seams or weaving in ends, it is necessary to cut knots made at ends of yarn.

Place fronts with wrong sides facing you. Fold bottom 8" of each front up to form pocket **(Fig 8)**. Using overcast stitch (see page 22), sew center edge of each pocket **(Fig 8)**.

Turn pockets to right side and pin top edge and side openings of each pocket to hold in place.

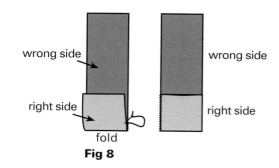

Fig 8

Pin fronts and back with right sides together at shoulders, leaving about 6" (6", 7", 8", 8½", 9") of center back open for neckline. Starting at armhole edge, sew shoulder seams using overcast stitch. Open flat **(Fig 9)**.

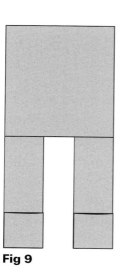

Fig 9

Measure down 10" (10", 11", 11", 12½", 12½") from shoulder seam on back and each front and mark with pins; mark center of bound off edge of each sleeve **(Fig 10)**. With right sides together, pin center of one sleeve to shoulder seam. Pin one edge of sleeve to marker on back and other edge of sleeve to marker on front. Sew in place using overcast stitch. Repeat for remaining sleeve.

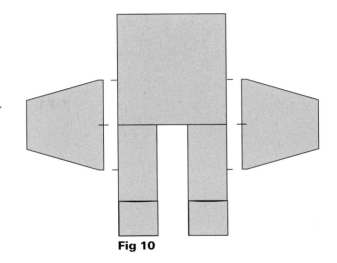

Fig 10

Place front and back with right sides together, and right sides of sleeves together **(Fig 11)**. Pin edges together, making sure pocket is between front and back. Sew side and sleeve seams, being sure to catch edge of pocket into side seam.

Carefully weave in all loose yarn ends on wrong side of sweater.

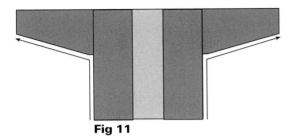

Fig 11

Hug Me Sweater

This wonderful warm sweater is as good as a hug from your favorite person. It has a loose, easy fit with a comfortable, rolled collar.

We've made our models in Lion Brand® Imagine, a cuddly-soft yarn that wraps you in warmth. It works up quickly because you knit with two strands of yarn at the same time.

Sound difficult? It's not; just knit or purl, being sure to work both strands at the same time.

Hint: Although it is worked with strands from two different skeins held together, don't be tempted to wind the two skeins into one ball. Use the yarn just as it comes from the skeins. Be sure to keep your tension the same on both strands.

Follow the instructions for this fun-to-knit sweater, then choose to assemble it with either the purl side (like the lower right sweater) or the knit side (like the upper left sweater) to the outside.

Shown in color photograph on page 27.

Sizing:

This sweater has an easy comfortable fit, with 4" to 8" allowed for ease.

Note: Pattern is written for size medium with changes for other sizes in parentheses.

Size	Body Measurement at Bust	Finished Garment Measurement at Bust
Medium	34"-38"	46"
Large	40"-44"	50"
X-Large	46"-50"	54"

All measurements are approximate.

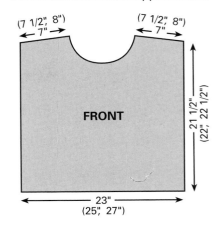

FRONT

(7 1/2", 8")
← 7" →

(7 1/2", 8")
← 7" →

21 1/2"
(22", 22 1/2")

23"
(25", 27")

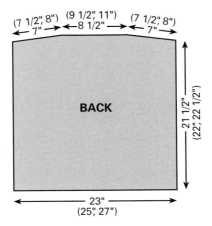

BACK

(7 1/2", 8")
← 7" →

(9 1/2", 11")
← 8 1/2" →

(7 1/2", 8")
← 7" →

21 1/2"
(22", 22 1/2")

23"
(25", 27")

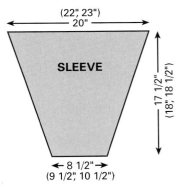

SLEEVE

(22", 23")
20"

17 1/2"
(18", 18 1/2")

← 8 1/2" →
(9 1/2", 10 1/2")

Materials:

Lion Brand® Imagine worsted weight yarn in 2.5-oz pull skeins in color of your choice (we have used Maize, Color 186; Blue Heather, Color 111; and Autumn Leaves, Color 325 for our models)

6 skeins for size Medium
7 skeins for size Large
8 skeins for size X-Large

Equipment:

Size 13, 29" circular knitting needle, or size required for gauge.
Size I aluminum crochet hook (for correcting mistakes and picking up stitches)
Two 6¼" long stitch holders
Size 13 steel tapestry sewing needle, or plastic yarn needle
Straight pins

Gauge:

In Stockinette Stitch (knit one row, purl one row) with 2 strands of yarn, 5 stitches = 2" (measure gauge on reverse or purl side)

Making the Gauge Swatch:

To be sure the sweater will be the correct size, begin by making a sample swatch that will let you measure your gauge, as well as give you some practice working with two strands of yarn and a circular needle.

Take two skeins of yarn and hold two strands together.

With both strands, cast on 20 stitches. Turn needle so that cast-on stitches are in left hand and last stitch cast-on is first stitch to be worked.

Row 1:

Being careful to use both strands at the same time, purl every stitch.

Row 2:

Being careful to use both strands at the same time, knit every stitch.

Repeat Rows 1 and 2 until you feel comfortable with the work, and your stitches are even. Work at least 18 rows. Loosely bind off all stitches. Then place the gauge swatch on a flat surface, and measure in center of swatch to see if the stitches are worked to gauge. There should be 5 stitches in every two inches (see **photo**). If you do not have 5 stitches in every two inches, see Lesson 8 on page 19.

When the gauge is just right, you're ready to start the sweater.

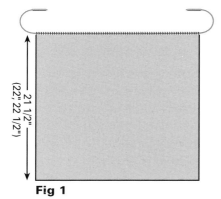
5 stitches = 2 inches

(Reverse side of stockinette stitch)

Sweater Instructions

Note: Pattern is written for size medium with changes for other sizes in parentheses. It is also written with the purl side as the right side. When assembling your sweater, you may choose to have the knit side as the right side.

Back

With 2 strands of yarn held together, cast on 58 (62, 68) stitches. Turn needle so that cast-on stitches are in left hand and last stitch cast-on is first to be worked.

Row 1 (right side of garment):
Purl each stitch.

Row 2:
Knit each stitch.

Repeat Rows 1 and 2 until piece measures 21½" (22", 22½") from the cast-on row (see **Fig 1**). This is the length the sweater will be to the shoulders.

The last row worked should be a purl row, so if you finished with a knit row, now purl one more row.

21 1/2"
(22", 22 1/2")

Fig 1

Shoulder Shaping:

Now we'll shape the shoulders by binding off several stitches at the beginning of each the next four rows.

Shoulder Row 1:

Loosely bind off the first 9 (9, 10) stitches as to knit (**Figs 2**, **3** and **4**); then knit the remaining stitches.

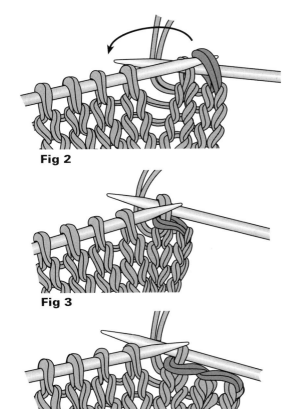

Fig 2

Fig 3

Fig 4

Shoulder Row 2:

Loosely bind off the first 9 (9, 10) stitches as to purl (**Figs 5**, **6** and **7**); then purl the remaining stitches.

Stop and count your stitches; there should be 40 (44, 48) stitches on your needle.

Shoulder Row 3:

Loosely bind off the first 9 (10, 10) stitches as to knit; then knit the remaining stitches.

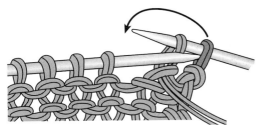

Fig 5

Fig 6

Fig 7

Shoulder Row 4:

Loosely bind off the first 9 (10, 10) stitches as to purl; then purl the remaining stitches.

There should now be 22 (24, 28) stitches on your needle. These stitches will be used later to form the back of the neck. We're not going to bind off these stitches; instead we are going to safely set them aside. So take a 6 1/4" stitch holder, and slip the remaining stitches on it (Fig 8). Close the stitch holder. Cut the yarn, leaving 6" yarn ends and set piece aside.

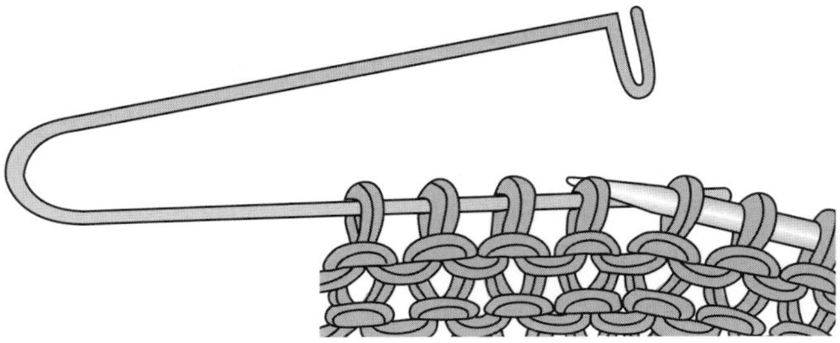

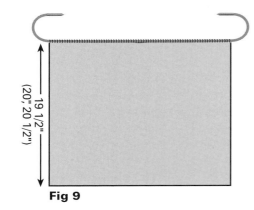

Fig 8

Front

Work the same way as the Back until piece measures 19 1/2" (20", 20 1/2") from the cast-on edge (Fig 9). Measure in same manner as the Back. Purl one row if needed to end by working a purl row.

Note: We worked this piece 2" shorter than the back to allow for the front neckline, which is lower than the back neckline.

On the next row, you will place the stitches reserved for the neck onto the second 6 1/4" stitch holder to be worked later. Now you will work both shoulders at the same time, but each shoulder will be worked with separate yarn.

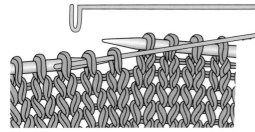

19 1/2" (20", 20 1/2")

Fig 9

Neckline Shaping:

Neckline Row 1 (wrong side of garment):
Knit the first 26 (27, 29) sts (which will become the Right Shoulder); now drop the two strands of yarn; slip the next 6 (8, 10) stitches (which will become the front neck) onto a 6 1/4" stitch holder (Fig 10); close the stitch holder and drop it; join two new strands of yarn by inserting needle in first stitch to be worked with new yarn; loop new yarn around needle leaving a 6" end or longer (Fig 11); draw loop through stitch on needle; knit the remaining stitches (which will become the Left Shoulder).

Neckline Row 2:
Purl the first 26 (27, 29) stitches; drop the two strands of working yarn; pick up the working yarn on Right Shoulder and working on Right Shoulder stitches, bind off the first 4 stitches as to purl; purl the remaining stitches.

Neckline Row 3:
Knit the first 22 (23, 25) stitches; drop the working yarn; pick up the working yarn on other shoulder and working other shoulder stitches, bind off the first 4 stitches as to knit; knit the remaining stitches.

You should now have 22 (23, 25) stitches on each shoulder.

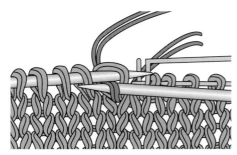

Fig 10

Fig 11

Neckline Row 4:
Purl the first 22 (23, 25) stitches; drop the working yarn, and pick up the working yarn on other shoulder; bind off the first 4 (4, 5) stitches as to purl; purl the remaining stitches.

Neckline Row 5:
Knit the first 18 (19, 20) stitches; drop the working yarn, and pick up the working yarn on other shoulder; bind off the first 4 (4, 5) stitches as to knit; knit the remaining stitches.

You should now have 18 (19, 20) stitches on each shoulder.

Neckline Row 6:
Purl the first 18 (19, 20) stitches; drop working yarn, and pick up the yarn on other shoulder; purl next 18 (19, 20) stitches.

Measure on flat surface as before. Straight unshaped outer edges should measure 21½" (22", 22½") from cast-on edge **(Fig 12)**. If necessary, knit one row; then purl one row to reach measurement.

Shoulder Shaping:
Now we'll shape the shoulders by binding off several stitches at the beginning of the next 4 rows.

Shoulder Row 1:
Bind off first 9 (9, 10) stitches as to knit; knit the remaining stitches; drop working yarn, and pick up yarn on other shoulder; knit next 18 (19, 20) stitches.

Shoulder Row 2:
Bind off first 9 (9, 10) stitches as to purl; purl remaining stitches; drop working yarn and pick up yarn on other shoulder; purl next 9 (10, 10) stitches.

You should now have 9 (10, 10) stitches on each shoulder.

Shoulder Row 3:
Bind off first 9 (10, 10) stitches as to knit; drop working yarn and pick up yarn on other shoulder; knit remaining 9 (10, 10) stitches on other shoulder.

Shoulder Row 4:
Bind off all stitches as to purl.

Cut yarn, leaving 6" yarn ends and set piece aside.

Sleeves (make 2)
With two strands of yarn, cast on 22 (24, 26) stitches.

Row 1 (right side of garment):
Purl each stitch.

Row 2:
Knit each stitch.

Row 3:
Purl each stitch.

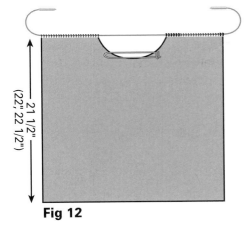

Fig 12

21 1/2" (22", 22 1/2")

Row 4:

Knit the first stitch, increase by knitting in front and back of next stitch **(Figs 13** and **14)**; knit to last 2 stitches; increase by knitting in front and back of next stitch; knit last stitch.

Repeat Rows 1 through 4 in sequence 12 times more.

You should now have 48 **(50, 52)** stitches.

For size medium only:

Repeat Rows 3 and 4 of sleeve once more.

You should now have 50 stitches. Continue with "For All Sizes" below.

For sizes large and X-large only:

Repeat Rows 3 and 4 of sleeve three times more.

You should now have 56 stitches for size large and 58 stitches for size X-large. Continue with "For All Sizes" below.

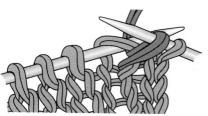

Fig 13

Fig 14

For All Sizes:

Repeat Rows 1 and 2 of sleeve until piece measures 17½" **(18", 18½")** from cast-on edge **(Fig 15)**, end by working a Row 2.

Bind off all stitches as to purl.

Cut yarn, leaving 6" yarn ends and set piece aside.

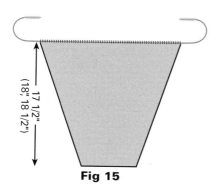

Fig 15

Collar

Before knitting the collar, it is necessary to sew the shoulder seams. At this point you will need to decide which side you wish to have as the right side of your garment. Place back and front flat as shown **(Fig 16)**. Referring to Lesson 10 on page 21, weave shoulder seams.

Now you will work the collar in one piece.

You begin by "picking up" stitches along the shaped front neck edges, and knitting the stitches from the holders back onto the circular needle.

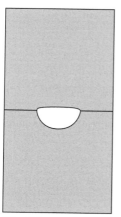

Fig 16

Hold sweater with right side facing you and neckline at top.

Pick up 12 (14, 14) stitches down left side of neck edge (Figs 17 and 18); knit next 6 (8, 10) stitches from front holder; pick up 12 (14, 14) stitches up right side of neck edge; knit remaining 22 (24, 28) stitches from back holder.

You should have 52 (60, 66) stitches.

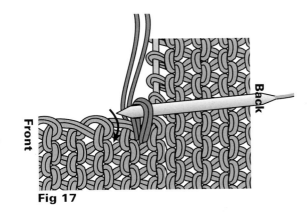

Fig 17

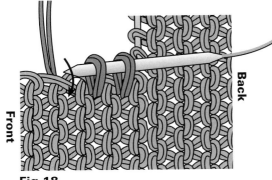

Fig 18

Fig 19

Note: Now it is necessary to place a marker (either a purchased plastic one or a loop of yarn) on the needle before knitting the first stitch to mark the beginning of the round.

The collar is made in one piece by working in rounds. (This means after working all stitches, do not turn needle; slip the marker and continue working in same direction.) All rounds are knitted.

You will begin the first round by working in the first stitch you picked up along the left-hand side of neck edge (**Fig 19**).

Round 1:
Knit each stitch.

Rounds 2 through 11:
Repeat Round 1.

Loosely bind off all stitches as to knit.

Collar will roll naturally to right side of sweater.

Finishing

Note: Refer to Lesson 10 on page 21 for information on joining seams and weaving in ends.

Open joined piece out on a flat surface. Measure down 10" (11", 11½") from shoulder seam on both sides of front and back and mark with pins; mark center of bound off edge of each sleeve in same manner **(Fig 20)**.

Match marked centers of sleeves to shoulder seam and edge of sleeves to marked points on front and back of sweater. Weave each sleeve in place.

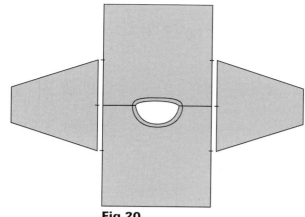

Fig 20

Place front and back with side seams and sleeve edges together. Weave side and sleeve seams **(Fig 21)** in continuous seam in direction as shown **(Fig 22)**.

Carefully weave in all loose yarn ends on wrong side of garment.

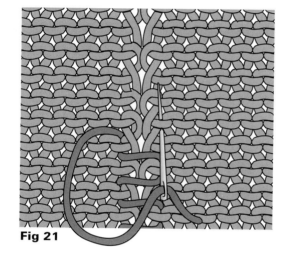

Fig 21

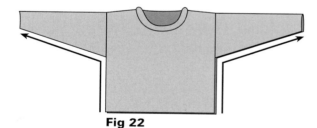

Fig 22

Quick Cardigan

Whether you're wearing jeans or a dressy silk skirt, you can depend on this cardigan for a cozy layer of warmth. You'll love to see how quickly you make progress when knitting with this Lion Brand® chunky weight yarn called Wool-Ease® Thick & Quick. It's a toasty acrylic with some wool blended in for luxurious body and warmth.

Follow the instructions for making this sweater then choose to assemble it with either the rib side (like lower right sweater) or the reversed pebble side (like upper left sweater) to the outside.

Shown in color photograph on back cover.

Sizing:

The cardigan has an easy, comfortable fit, with 8" to 10" allowed for ease. It is designed to be worn open at the front.

Note: Pattern is written for size small with changes for other sizes in parentheses.

Size	Body Measurement at Bust	Finished Garment Measurement at Bust
Small	30"-32"	40"
Meduim	34"-36"	44"
Large	38"-40"	48"
1X	42"-44"	52"
2X	46"-48"	56"
3X	50"-52"	60"

All measurements are approximate.

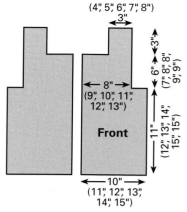

Front

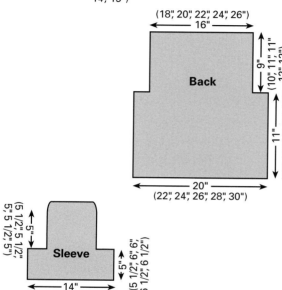

Back

Sleeve

Materials:

Lion Brand® Wool-Ease® chunky weight yarn in 6-oz pull skeins in color of your choice (we used Pewter, Color 152; Wood, Color 404; and Fisherman, Color 099 for our models)

5 skeins for size Small
6 skeins for size Medium
7 skeins for size Large
7 skeins for size 1X
8 skeins for size 2X
8 skeins for size 3X

Equipment:

Size 17, 14" straight knitting needles or size required for gauge
Size 10½", 14" straight knitting needles (for neck edging)
Size J aluminum crochet hook (for correcting mistakes and picking up stitches)
Two 4½" long stitch holders
Size 13 steel tapestry sewing needle, or plastic yarn needle
Straight pins

Gauge:

Worked in ribbed pattern below, 2 stitches = 1"

Ribbed Pattern:

Pattern Row 1 (right side of garment):
* Knit 1 stitch, purl 1 stitch * ; repeat instructions between the *s across row to last stitch; knit last stitch.

Pattern Row 2:
Purl each stitch.

Repeat Rows 1 and 2 to create the pattern.

Making the Gauge Swatch:

To be sure the sweater will be the correct size, begin by making a sample swatch that will let you measure your gauge, as well as give you some practice working with bulky weight yarn.

With larger size needles, cast on 18 stitches.

Repeat Ribbed Pattern Rows 1 and 2 until you feel comfortable with the work, and your stitches are even. Work at least 16 rows. Bind off all stitches. Then place the gauge swatch on a flat surface, and measure in center of swatch to see if the stitches are worked to gauge. There should be 2 stitches in every inch (see **photo**). If you do not have the 2 stitches in every inch, see Lesson 8 on page 19.

When the gauge is just right, you're ready to start the cardigan.

2 stitches = 1 inch

Cardigan Instructions

Note: Pattern is written for size small with changes for other sizes in parentheses. It is also written with the ribbed side as the right side. When assembling your sweater, you may choose to have the pebbled side as the right side.

Back

With larger size needles, cast on 41 (45, 49, 53, 57, 61) stitches.

Row 1 (right side of garment):
* Knit 1 stitch, purl 1 stitch * ; repeat instructions between the *s across row to last stitch; knit last stitch.

Row 2:
Purl each stitch.

Repeat Rows 1 and 2 until piece measures 11" (12", 13", 14", 15", 15") from cast-on edge (**Fig 1**), end by working a wrong side row (**Row 2**). For ease in measuring later, mark this row by tying a short length of yarn in the first and last stitch.

Now we will shape the armholes by binding off several stitches at the beginning of each of the next 2 rows.

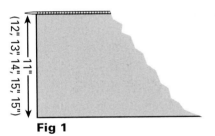

11" (12", 13", 14", 15", 15")

Fig 1

Armhole Shaping:
Armhole Shaping Row 1:
Bind off first 4 stitches as to knit (**Figs 2**, **3** and **4)**; ***** purl 1 stitch, knit 1 stitch *****; repeat instructions between the *****s across.

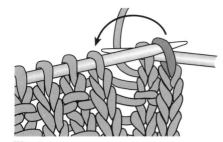

Fig 2

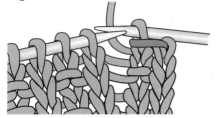

Fig 3

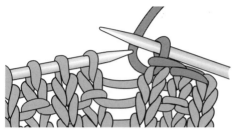

Fig 4

Armhole Shaping Row 2:
Bind off first 4 stitches as to purl (**Figs 5**, **6** and **7)**; purl remaining stitches.

You should have 33 (**37, 41, 45, 49, 53)** stitches on your needle.

Armhole Shaping Row 3:
* Knit 1 stitch, purl 1 stitch *****; repeat instructions between the *****s to last stitch; knit last stitch.

Armhole Shaping Row 4:
Purl each stitch.

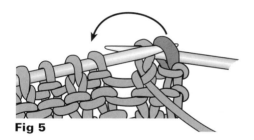

Fig 5

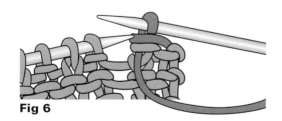

Fig 6

Fig 7

48

Repeat Armhole Shaping Rows 3 and 4 until armhole depth measures 9" (10", 11", 11", 12", 12") from marked row (Fig 8).

Note: To measure armhole depth, place piece on a flat surface; measure from the center of row marked with yarn to the work on the needle.

Repeat Armhole Shaping Row 3.

Bind off all stitches as to purl.

Cut yarn, leaving a 6" yarn end and set piece aside.

Now we will work each front section separately. Remember the terms for left and right refer to the piece as it is worn (see "Terms" on page 20).

Left Front

With larger size needles, cast on 21 (23, 25, 27, 29, 31) stitches.

Left Front Row 1 (right side of garment):
* Knit 1 stitch, purl 1 stitch *; repeat instructions between *s to last stitch; knit last stitch.

Left Front Row 2:
Purl each stitch.

Repeat Left Front Rows 1 and 2 until piece measures 11" (12", 13", 14", 15", 15") from cast-on edge (Fig 9), end by working a wrong side row (Row 2). Mark this row by tying a short length of yarn in last stitch.

Now we will shape the armhole by binding off several stitches at the beginning of the next row.

Armhole Shaping:
Armhole Shaping Row 1:
Bind off first 4 stitches as to knit; * purl 1 stitch, knit 1 stitch *; repeat instructions between *s across.

Armhole Shaping Row 2:
Purl each stitch.

You should now have 17 (19, 21, 23, 25, 27) stitches.

Armhole Shaping Row 3:
* Knit 1 stitch, purl 1 stitch *; repeat instructions between *s to last stitch; knit last stitch.

Armhole Shaping Row 4:
Purl each stitch.

Repeat Armhole Shaping Rows 3 and 4 until piece measures 6" (7", 8", 8", 9", 9") from beginning of armhole shaping (Fig 10).

Repeat Armhole Shaping Row 3.

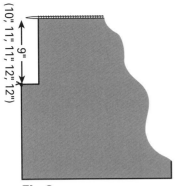

Fig 8

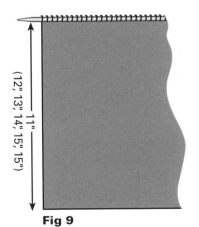

Fig 9

Fig 10

49

Now we will shape the neck edge.

Neck Shaping:
Neck Shaping Row 1:
Purl first 8 stitches, and slip these to a stitch holder **(Fig 11)**; purl remaining stitches.

You should now have 9 **(11, 13, 15, 17, 19)** stitches.

Neck Shaping Row 2:
* Knit 1 stitch, purl 1 stitch *****; repeat instructions between *****s to last stitch; knit last stitch.

Neck Shaping Row 3:
Bind off 1 stitch as to purl; purl remaining stitches.

Neck Shaping Row 4:
* Knit 1 stitch, purl 1 stitch *****; repeat instructions between *****s across.

Neck Shaping Row 5:
Repeat Neck Shaping Row 3.

You should now have 7 **(9, 11, 13, 15, 17)** stitches.

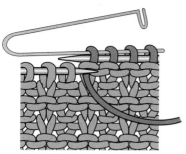

Fig 11

Now we will work the shoulder section.

Shoulder:
Row 1:
* Knit 1 stitch, purl 1 stitch *****; repeat instructions between *****s to last stitch; knit last stitch.

Row 2:
Purl each stitch.

Repeat Rows 1 and 2 until piece measures 9" (10", 11", 11", 12", 12") from bound off stitches on armhole shaping **(Fig 12)**, end by working a right side row (Row 1).

Bind off all stitches as to purl.

Cut yarn, leaving a 6" yarn end and set piece aside.

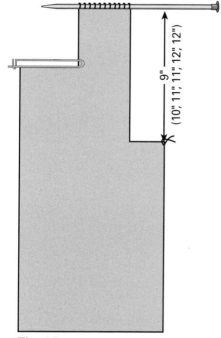

Fig 12

Right Front

With larger size needles, cast on 21 (23, 25, 27, 29, 31) stitches.

Right Front Row 1 (right side of garment**):**
* Knit 1 stitch, purl 1 stitch *; repeat instructions between *s to last stitch; knit last stitch.

Right Front Row 2:
Purl each stitch.

Repeat Right Front Rows 1 and 2, until piece measures 11" (12", 13", 14", 15", 15") from cast-on edge **(Fig 13)**, end by working a wrong side row **(**Row 2**)**. Mark this row by tying a short length of yarn in first stitch.

Note: Count the number of rows on right front piece to be sure you have the same number as on left front piece.

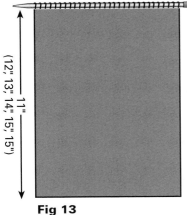

Fig 13

Now we will shape the armhole.

Armhole Shaping:
Armhole Shaping Row 1:
* Knit 1 stitch, purl 1 stitch *; repeat instructions between *s to last stitch; knit last stitch.

Armhole Shaping Row 2:
Bind off first 4 stitches as to purl; purl remaining stitches.

You should now have 17 (19, 21, 23, 25, 27) stitches.

Armhole Shaping Row 3:
* Knit 1 stitch, purl 1 stitch *; repeat instructions between *s to last stitch; knit last stitch.

Armhole Shaping Row 4:
Purl each stitch.

Repeat Armhole Shaping Rows 3 and 4 until piece measures 6" (7", 8", 8", 9", 9") from beginning of armhole shaping **(Fig 14)**.

Repeat Armhole Shaping Row 3.

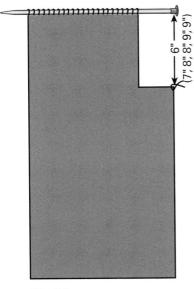

Fig 14

Now we will shape the neck edge.

Neck Shaping:
Neck Shaping Row 1:
Purl next 9 (11, 13, 15, 17, 19); slip next 8 stitches to a stitch holder to work later (**Fig15**).

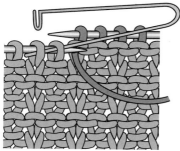
Fig 15

Neck Shaping Row 2:
Bind off 1 stitch as to knit; * knit 1 stitch, purl 1 stitch *; repeat instructions between *s to last stitch; knit last stitch.

Neck Shaping Row 3:
Purl each stitch.

Neck Shaping Row 4:
Bind off 1 stitch as to purl; * purl 1 stitch, knit 1 stitch *; repeat instructions between *s across.

You should now have 7 (9, 11, 13, 15, 17) stitches.

Neck Shaping Row 5:
Purl each stitch.

Now we will work the shoulder section.

Shoulder:
Row 1:
* Knit 1 stitch, purl 1 stitch *; repeat instructions between *s to last stitch; knit last stitch.

Row 2:
Purl each stitch.

Repeat Rows 1 and 2 until piece measures 9" (10", 11", 11", 12", 12") from bound off stitches on armhole shaping (**Fig 16**), end by working a right side row (Row 1).

Bind off all stitches as to purl.

Cut yarn, leaving a 6" yarn end and set work aside.

Sleeve (make 2)
With larger needles, cast on 29 (31, 35, 37, 39, 41) stitches.
Row 1 (right side of garment):
* Knit 1 stitch, purl 1 stitch *; repeat instructions between *s to last stitch; knit last stitch.

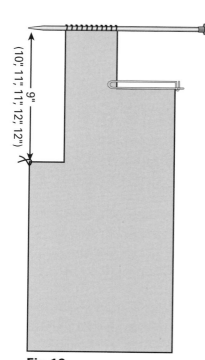
Fig 16

Row 2:
Purl each stitch.

Repeat Rows 1 and 2 until sleeve measures 5" (5 1/2", 6", 6", 6 1/2", 6 1/2") from cast-on edge (**Fig 17**), end with a wrong side row (Row 2). For ease in measuring later, mark this row by tying a short length of yarn in the first and last stitch.

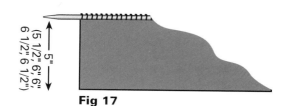
Fig 17

Now we will shape the armhole.

Armhole Shaping:
Armhole Shaping Row 1:
Bind off first 4 stitches as to knit **(Figs 18**, **19** and **20)**; ***** purl 1 stitch, knit 1 stitch *****; repeat instructions between *****s across.

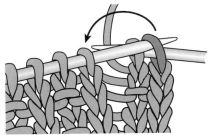

Fig 18

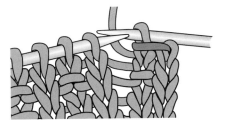

Fig 19

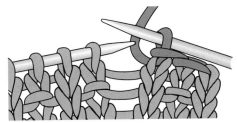

Fig 20

Armhole Shaping Row 2:
Bind off first 4 stitches as to purl **(Figs 21**, **22** and **23)**; purl remaining stitches.

You should now have 21 **(**23, 27, 29, 31, 33**)** stitches.

Armhole Shaping Row 3:
* Knit 1 stitch, purl 1 stitch *****; repeat instructions between *****s to last stitch; knit last stitch.

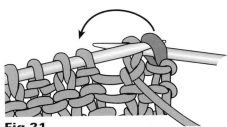

Fig 21

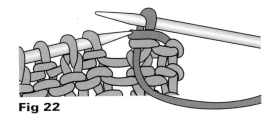

Fig 22

Fig 23

Armhole Shaping Row 4:

Purl each stitch.

Repeat Armhole Shaping Rows 3 and 4 until piece measures 5" (5½", 5½", 5", 5½", 5") from bound off stitches **(Fig 24)**, end with a wrong side row **(Armhole Shaping Row 4)**.

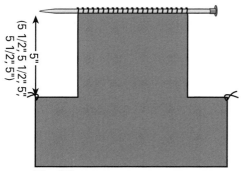

Fig 24

Cap Shaping:
Cap Shaping Row 1:

Knit 1 stitch, decrease by knitting next 2 stitches together **(Figs 25** and **26)**; * purl 1 stitch, knit 1 stitch *; repeat instructions between *s to last 3 stitches; decrease by knitting next 2 stitches together; knit last stitch.

Fig 25

Fig 26

Cap Shaping Row 2:

Purl 1 stitch, decrease by purling next 2 stitches together **(Fig 27)**; purl to last 3 stitches; decrease by purling next 2 stitches together; purl last stitch.

Cap Shaping Row 3:

Knit 1 stitch, decrease by knitting next 2 stitches together; knit 1 stitch; * purl 1 stitch, knit 1 stitch; repeat instructions between *s to last 3 stitches; decrease by knitting next 2 stitches together; knit last stitch.

You should now have 15 (17, 21, 23, 25, 27) stitches.

Bind off all stitches as to purl.

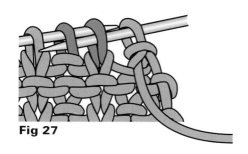

Fig 27

Before knitting the neck ribbing it is necessary to sew the shoulder seams. At this point you will need to decide which side you wish to have as the right side of your garment. Place back and front out on a flat surface as shown **(Fig 28)**. Referring Lesson 10 page 21, weave shoulder seams, leaving center 19 stitches unused for back neck opening.

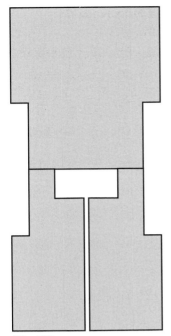

Fig 28

Neck Ribbing:

With right side facing you and smaller size needles, knit 8 stitches from right neck holder; pick up 8 **(8, 9, 9, 10, 10)** stitches along right neck edge **(Fig 29)**; pick up 19 stitches across bound off stitches along back neck edge **(Fig 30)**; pick up 8 **(8, 9, 9, 10, 10)** stitches along left neck edge; slip the 8 stitches from stitch holder to second needle; knit the 8 stitches from second needle.

You should now have 51 **(51, 53, 53, 55, 55)** stitches on needle.

Neck Ribbing Row 1:

* Knit 1 stitch, purl 1 stitch *****; repeat instructions between *****s to last stitch; knit last stitch.

Neck Ribbing Row 2:

* Purl 1 stitch, knit 1 stitch *****; repeat instructions between *****s across to last stitch; purl last stitch.

Repeat Rows 1 and 2 until neck ribbing measures 1¹/2".

Bind off all stitches in pattern.

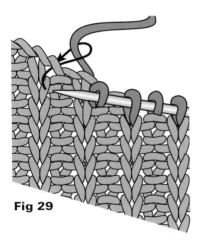

Fig 29

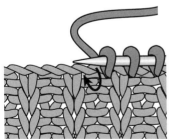

Fig 30

Finishing

Note: Refer to Lesson 10 on page 21 for information on joining seams and weaving in ends.

With pins, mark center of bound off edge of each sleeve.

Open piece flat and place sleeves in armhole openings, matching marked center top of sleeve to shoulder seam, and bound off stitches at underarm **(Fig 31)**. Weave sleeves in place, easing sleeve cap to fit armhole opening.

Matching side and sleeve seams, weave side and sleeve edges in continuous seam in direction as shown **(Fig 32)**.

Carefully weave in all loose yarn ends on wrong side of garment.

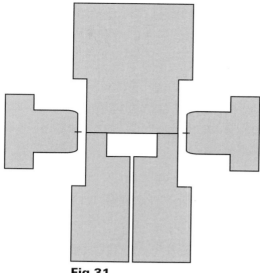

Fig 31

Fig 32

Stripe It Rich Sweater

This garment is worked in Wool-Ease®, a soft wool and acrylic neatly woven, light-weight worsted yarn. It is worked in an interesting three-color striped pattern with added texture. But you don't have to dread weaving in all those yarn ends from the color changes; the colors change every two rows so that you can loosely carry unused yarns up the sides until they are needed again. The sweater is fun to knit and great to wear. Make it in any combination of three complimentary colors— soft, pastel shades, dramatic darks, or cheerful brights. Wool-Ease® is available in over 50 colors.

Shown in color photograph on page 28.

Sizing:

The sweater has an easy comfortable fit, with 6" allowed for ease.

Note: Pattern is written for size small with changes for other sizes in parentheses.

Size	Body Measurement at Bust	Finished Garment Measurement at Bust
Small	30"-32"	38"
Medium	34"-36"	42"
Large	38"-40"	46"
1X	42"-44"	50"
2X	46"-48"	54"
3X	50"-52"	58"

All measurements are approximate.

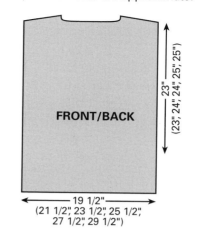

FRONT/BACK

23" (23", 24", 24", 25", 25")

19 1/2" (21 1/2", 23 1/2", 25 1/2", 27 1/2", 29 1/2")

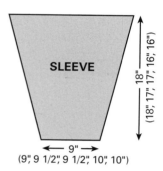

SLEEVE

18" (18", 17", 17", 16", 16")

9" (9", 9 1/2", 9 1/2", 10", 10")

Materials:

Lion Brand® Wool-Ease® worsted weight yarn in 3-oz pull skeins—Color A-#99 Fisherman, 3 (3,3,3,4,4) skeins; Color B-#130 Green Heather, 2 (2,3,3,3,3) skeins; Color C-#179 Chestnut Heather or #140 Rose Heather, 2 (2,3,3,3,3) skeins

Equipment:

Size 8, 14" straight knitting needles, or size required for gauge
Size G aluminum crochet hook (for correcting mistakes and picking up stitches).
Three 6¾" long stitch holders
Size 16 steel tapestry sewing needle, or plastic yarn needle
Straight pins

Gauge:

In stockinette stitch (knit one row; purl one row), 4 stitches = 1"

Making the Gauge Swatch:

To be sure the sweater will be the correct size, begin by making a sample swatch that will let you measure your gauge.
Cast on 20 stitches.

Row 1:
Knit each stitch.

Row 2:
Purl each stitch.

Repeat Rows 1 and 2 ten times more. Loosely bind off all stitches as to knit. Then place gauge swatch on a flat surface, and measure in center of swatch to see if the stitches are worked to gauge. There should be 4 stitches in every one inch (see **photo**). If you do not have 4 stitches in every inch, refer to Lesson 8 on page 19.

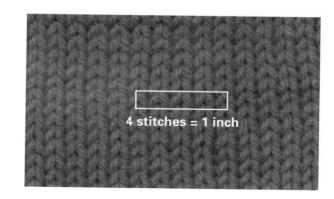

4 stitches = 1 inch

Striped Pattern:

Color A—Fisherman

Color B—Green Heather

Color C—Chestnut Heather or Rose Heather

Row 1 (right side):
With Color B, knit.

Row 2:
With Color B, purl.

Row 3:
With Color C, knit.

Row 4:
With Color C, purl.

Row 5:
With Color A, knit.

Row 6:
With Color A, knit.

Rows 7 and 8:
Repeat Rows 3 and 4.

Rows 9 and 10:
Repeat Rows 1 and 2.

Rows 11 and 12:
Repeat Rows 5 and 6.

This completes one pattern sequence. Repeat Rows 1 through 12 to create the pattern.

Sweater Instructions

Note: Yarn is carried along edge of sweater. When changing to a new color at the beginning of the row, bring the new color under the old color. When carrying the old color along edge, bring the working color under the old color at the beginning of the row to lock it in place **(Fig 1)**.

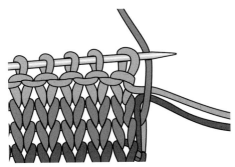

Fig 1

Back

Bottom Border:
With Color A, cast on 78 (86, 94, 102, 110, 118) stitches.

Row 1 (right side of garment):
Knit each stitch.

Rows 2 through 6:
Repeat Row 1.

Body:
Work in Striped Pattern until piece measures 23" (23", 24", 24", 25", 25") from cast-on edge **(Fig 2)**, end by working either a Striped Pattern Row 6 or a Striped Pattern Row 12.

Note: For the color sequence to fall correctly at the neckline, the last row you work must be either a Striped Pattern Row 6 or a Striped Pattern Row 12. If necessary, work additional rows so you end by working a Row 6 or a Row 12.

Shoulder and Neck Shaping:
Now we'll shape the shoulders and neck edge.

Note: On the next row, you will divide the work, first working the First Shoulder stitches, then placing the Neck and Second

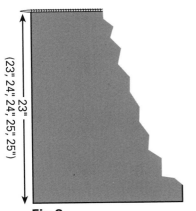

Fig 2

23"
(23", 24", 24", 25", 25")

Shoulder stitches on holders to be worked later. Be sure to keep work in the color pattern sequence already established.

First Shoulder Row 1 (right side of garment):
Bind off first 5 (6, 7, 8, 8, 9) stitches as to knit (**Figs 3**, **4** and **5**);

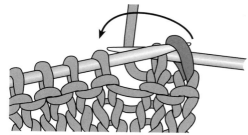

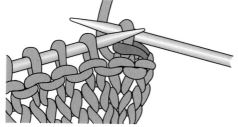

Fig 3

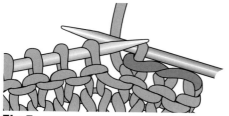

Fig 4

Fig 5

knit next 16 (18, 20, 22, 25, 28) stitches for First Shoulder; place next 34 (36, 38, 40, 42, 42) stitches on a holder for Neck (**Fig 6**), close this holder; place remaining 22 (25, 28, 31, 34, 38) stitches on another holder for Second Shoulder.

Now work only on First Shoulder, and continue to change colors as needed.

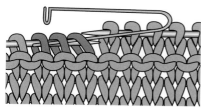

Fig 6

60

Perfect Pullover

This will quickly become your favorite outdoor wear-over-everything sweater. It has a V-neck that looks good with either a turtleneck, a T-shirt or a blouse. The sleeves are shaped at the underarm for a nice fit.

It's quick to knit in a Lion Brand® chunky weight yarn, called Wool-Ease® Thick & Quick. The yarn is spun with acrylic and enough wool blended to ensure you'll be toasty warm.

Follow the instructions for making this casual V-neck sweater, then choose to assemble it with either the rib side (like the lower left sweater) or the reversed pebble side (like the upper right sweater) to the outside.

Shown in color photograph on page 25.

Sizing:

The sweater has an easy comfortable fit, with 10" allowed for ease.

Note: Pattern is written for size small with changes for

Size	Body Measurement at Bust	Finished Garment Measurement at Bust
Small	30"-32"	44"
Medium	34"-36"	46"
Large	38"-40"	50"
1X	42"-44"	54"
2X	46"-48"	58"
3X	50"-52"	62"

Materials:

Lion Brand® Wool-Ease® Thick & Quick chunky weight yarn in 6-oz pull skeins in color of your choice (we have used Wheat, Color 402 and Pine, Color 182 for our models)

    7 skeins for size Small
    7 skeins for size Medium
    8 skeins for size Large
    8 skeins for size 1X
    9 skeins for size 2X
    9 skeins for size 3X

Equipment:

Size 11, 14" straight needles, or size required for gauge
Size H aluminum crochet hook (for correcting mistakes and
    picking up stitches)
Size 13 steel tapestry sewing needle, or plastic yarn needle

Gauge:

Worked in ribbed pattern below, 9 sts = 4"

Ribbed Pattern:

Pattern Row 1 (wrong side of the garment):
Knit the first stitch; ***** purl the next stitch, knit the next stitch *****; repeat the instructions between *****s across the row.
Pattern Row 2 (right side of the garment):
Knit each stitch.

Repeat Rows 1 and 2 to create the pattern.

Making the Gauge Swatch:

To be sure the sweater will be the correct size, begin by making a sample swatch that will let you measure your gauge, as well as give you some practice with the stitch and working with bulky yarn.

Cast on 22 stitches.

Repeat Ribbed Pattern Rows 1 and 2 four times (a total of 8 rows), then repeat Row 1 once. Then loosely bind off all stitches as to knit. Place gauge swatch on a flat surface, and measure in center of swatch to see if the stitches are worked to gauge. There should be 9 stitches in every four inches (see **photo**). If you do not have 9 stitches in every four inches, see Lesson 8 on page 19.

All measurements are approximate.

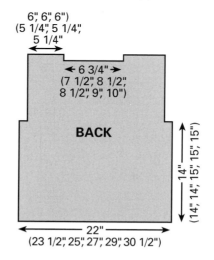

6", 6", 6")
(5 1/4", 5 1/4", 5 1/4")

← 6 3/4" →
(7 1/2", 8 1/2", 8 1/2", 9", 10")

BACK

14"
(14", 14", 15", 15", 15")

22"
(23 1/2", 25", 27", 29", 30 1/2")

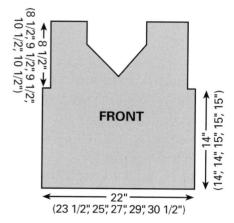

8 1/2"
(8 1/2", 9", 9 1/2", 9 1/2", 10 1/2", 10 1/2")

FRONT

14"
(14", 14", 15", 15", 15")

22"
(23 1/2", 25", 27", 29", 30 1/2")

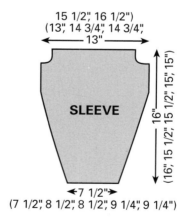

15 1/2", 16 1/2")
(13", 14 3/4", 14 3/4")
← 13" →

SLEEVE

16"
(16", 15 1/2", 15 1/2", 15", 15")

← 7 1/2" →
(7 1/2", 8 1/2", 8 1/2", 9 1/4", 9 1/4")

9 stitches = 4 inches

Sweater Instructions

Note: Pattern is written for size small with changes for other sizes in parentheses.

Back

Cast on 49 **(53, 57, 61, 65, 69)** stitches.

Row 1 (wrong side of garment**):**
Knit the first stitch; ***** purl the next stitch, knit the next stitch *****; repeat instructions between *****s across row.

Row 2 (right side of garment**):**
Knit each stitch.

Repeat Rows 1 and 2 until piece measures 14" **(**14", 14", 15", 15", 15"**)** from cast-on edge **(Fig 1)**, end by working a wrong side row (Row 1). This is the length of the sweater to the armholes. For ease in measuring later, mark this row by tying a short length of yarn in the first and last stitch of this row.

Note: Now you will begin decreasing to shape the armholes, the shoulders and the back of the neck. As you work the rest of the sweater, on the wrong side rows be sure to keep the stitches in the pattern as it has been established.

Armhole Shaping:
Armhole Shaping Row 1:

Bind off the first 2 **(**2, 2, 2, 2, 2**)** stitches as to knit **(Figs 2, 3** and **4)**; knit remaining stitches.

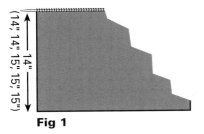

Fig 1

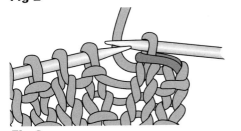

Fig 2

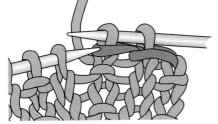

Fig 3

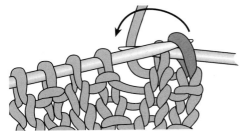

Fig 4

Armhole Shaping Row 2:
Bind off the first 2 (2, 2, 2, 2, 2) stitches as to purl (**Figs 5, 6** and **7**); ***** purl 1 stitch, knit 1 stitch *****; repeat instructions between *****s across row.

You should now have 45 (49, 53, 57, 61, 65) stitches on your needle.

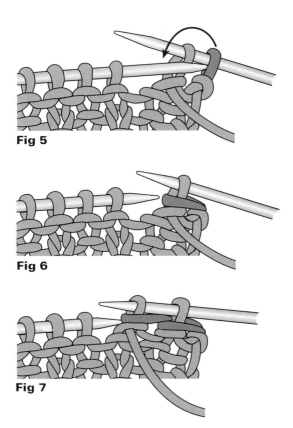

Fig 5

Fig 6

Fig 7

Armhole Shaping Row 3:
Decrease by knitting the first 2 stitches together (**Figs 8** and **9**), knit across row to last 2 stitches; decrease by knitting the last 2 stitches together.

You should now have 43 (47, 51, 55, 59, 63) stitches.

Armhole Shaping Row 4:
Purl 1 stitch; ***** knit 1 stitch, purl 1 stitch *****; repeat instructions between *****s across row.

Now you will work the next few rows differently depending on the size garment you are making.

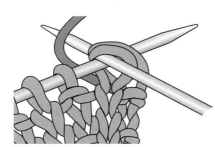

Fig 8

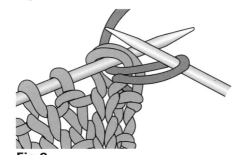

Fig 9

For size small only:

The shaping is complete and 43 stitches remain. Continue with "For All Sizes" on page 69.

For size medium only:

Working in pattern as established, repeat Armhole Shaping Rows 3 and 4 once more; 45 stitches remain. Continue with "For All Sizes" on page 69.

For sizes large and 1X only:

Working in pattern as established, repeat Armhole Shaping Rows 3 and 4 twice more; 47 stitches remain for size large and 51 stitches remain for size 1X. Continue with "For All Sizes" on page 69.

For size 2X only:

Working in pattern as established, repeat Armhole Shaping Rows 3 and 4 three times more; 53 stitches remain. Continue with "For All Sizes" below.

For size 3-X only:

Working in pattern as established, repeat Armhole Shaping Rows 3 and 4 four times more; 55 stitches remain. Continue with "For All Sizes" below.

For All Sizes:

Next Row:

Knit every stitch.

Work even in pattern as established (with no more decreases) until the armhole depth measures 8½" (8½", 9½", 9½", 10½", 10½"), end by working a wrong side row (**Fig 10**).

Note: To measure armhole depth, place piece on a flat surface; measure from the center of row marked with yarn to the work on the needle.

Now you will begin to shape the neck and the shoulders and you will work each shoulder with a separate skein of yarn.

Shape Neck and Shoulders:
Shaping Row 1:

Knit the first 13 (13, 13, 15, 15, 15) stitches for the Right Shoulder; now drop the yarn you have been working with, and join a new skein; with new yarn bind off as to knit the next 17 (19, 21, 21, 23, 25) stitches for the neck; knit across the remaining stitches for the Left Shoulder.

Shaping Row 2:

Work in pattern as established across the first 13 (13, 13, 15, 15, 15) stitches; drop working yarn; with working yarn of other shoulder, work in pattern as established across remaining stitches.

Shaping Row 3:

Bind off as to knit the first 13 (13, 13, 15, 15, 15) stitches; drop yarn; with other yarn, bind off as to knit the last 13 (13, 13, 15, 15, 15) stitches. Set piece aside.

Front

Work same as Back until piece measures same as back to beginning of armhole shaping. For ease in measuring later, mark last row worked by tying a short length of yarn in first and last stitch.

Armhole Shaping:
Armhole Shaping Row 1:

Bind off the first 2 (2, 2, 2, 2, 2) stitches as to knit; knit remaining stitches.

Armhole Shaping Row 2:

Bind off the first 2 (2, 2, 2, 2, 2) stitches as to purl; * purl 1 stitch, knit 1 stitch *; repeat instructions between *s across row.

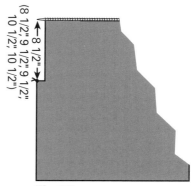

8½"
(8½", 9½", 9½", 10½", 10½")

Fig 10

You should now have 45 **(49, 53, 57, 61, 65)** stitches on your needle.

Armhole Shaping Row 3:
Decrease by knitting the first 2 stitches together; knit across row to last 2 stitches; decrease by knitting the last 2 stitches together.

You should now have 43 **(47, 51, 55, 59, 63)** stitches.

Armhole Shaping Row 4:
Work in pattern as established across row.

For size small only:

The shaping is complete and 43 stitches remain. Work in pattern as established until 8 rows have been worked from marked row, end by working a wrong side row. Continue with "V-neck Shaping" below.

For size medium only:

Repeat Rows 3 and 4 once more; 45 stitches remain. Work in pattern as established until 8 rows have been worked from marked row, end by working a wrong side row. Continue with "V-neck Shaping" below.

For sizes large, 1X, 2X and 3X only:

Repeat Rows 3 and 4 twice more; 47 stitches remain for size large, 51 stitches remain for size 1X, 55 sts remain for size 2X, and 59 sts remain for size 3X.

Continue with "V-neck Shaping" below.

V-neck Shaping:
Now you will begin to shape the V-neck, and you will work each side of the neck with a separate skein of yarn.

For sizes small, medium, large, and 1X only:

Shaping Row 1:
Knit across first 21 **(22, 23, 25)** stitches for Left Shoulder; drop working yarn; join a new skein; with new yarn bind off next stitch as to knit (this is center bottom of V-neck), knit across remaining stitches for Right Shoulder.

You should now have 21 **(22, 23, 25)** stitches on each shoulder.

Shaping Row 2:
Work in pattern as established across Right Shoulder; drop working yarn; with working yarn of Left Shoulder, bind off as to knit 1 stitch, work in pattern as established across remaining stitches.

Shaping Row 3:
Knit each stitch of Left Shoulder; drop yarn; with yarn of Right Shoulder, bind off as to knit 1 stitch; knit remaining stitches.

Continue with "For All Sizes" on page 71.

For size 2X only:

Shaping Row 1:

Decrease by knitting first 2 stitches together; knit next 25 stitches for Left Shoulder; drop working yarn; join a new skein; with new yarn, bind off next stitch as to knit (this is center bottom of V-neck), knit across Right Shoulder to last 2 sts; decrease by knitting the last 2 stitches together.

You should have 26 stitches on each shoulder.

Shaping Row 2:

Work in pattern as established across Right Shoulder; drop yarn; pick up yarn of Left Shoulder, bind off as to knit 1 stitch, work in pattern as established across remaining stitches.

Shaping Row 3:

Knit each stitch of Left Shoulder; drop working yarn; with yarn of Right Shoulder, bind off as to knit 1 stitch; knit remaining stitches.

You should have 25 stitches on each shoulder. Continue with "For All Sizes" below.

For 3X only:

Shaping Row 1:

Decrease by knitting first 2 stitches together; knit next 27 stitches for Left Shoulder; drop working yarn; join a new skein; with new yarn, bind off next stitch as to knit (this is center bottom of V-neck), knit across Right Shoulder to last 2 sts; decrease by knitting the last 2 stitches together.

You should have 28 stitches on each shoulder.

Shaping Row 2:

Work in pattern as established across Right Shoulder; drop yarn; pick up yarn of Left Shoulder, bind off as to knit 1 stitch, work in pattern as established across remaining stitches.

Shaping Row 3:

Decrease by knitting first 2 stitches together (decrease made); knit next 25 stitches of Left Shoulder; drop yarn; with yarn of Right Shoulder, bind off as to knit 1 stitch; knit across Right Shoulder to last 2 stitches; decrease by knitting last 2 stitches together.

You should now have 26 stitches on each shoulder.

Continue with "For All Sizes" below.

For All Sizes:

Shaping Row 4:

Work even in pattern as established across Right Shoulder; drop yarn; with yarn of Left Shoulder, bind off as to kint 1 stitch; work even in pattern as established across remaining stitches.

Shaping Row 5:

Knit each stitch of Left Shoulder; drop yarn; with yarn of Right Shoulder, bind off as to knit 1 stitch; knit remaining stitches.

Repeat Shaping Rows 4 and 5, 6 (7, 8, 8, 9, 10) times more.

You should now have 13 (13, 13, 15, 15, 15) stitches on each shoulder.

Work even in pattern as established until front measures same as back from armhole shaping, end by working a wrong side row.

Loosely bind off as to knit all stitches on each shoulder.

Sleeves (make 2)

Cast on 19 (19, 21, 21, 23, 23) stitches.

Row 1 (wrong side of garment):
Knit 1 stitch; * purl 1 stitch, knit 1 stitch *; repeat instructions between *s across row.

Row 2 (right side of garment):
Knit each stitch.

Row 3:
Repeat Row 1.

Row 4:
Knit first stitch, increase by knitting in front and back of next stitch (**Figs 11** and **12**); knit until 2 stitches remain; increase by knitting in front and back of next stitch; knit last stitch.

Row 5:
Knit 2 stitches; * purl 1 stitch, knit 1 stitch *; repeat instructions between *s across to last stitch; knit last stitch.

Row 6:
Knit each stitch.

Row 7:
Repeat Row 5.

Row 8:
Repeat Row 4.

Now you will work the next few rows differently depending on the size garment you are making.

Fig 11

Fig 12

For sizes small and medium only:

Rows 9 through 24:
Repeat Rows 1 through 8 twice more.

You should now have 31 stitches.

Row 25:
Knit 1 stitch; * purl 1 stitch, knit 1 stitch *; repeat instructions between *s across row.

Row 26:
Knit each stitch.

Row 27:
Repeat Row 25.

Row 28:
Knit each stitch.

Row 29:
Repeat Row 25.

Row 30:

Knit first stitch; increase in next stitch; knit until 2 stitches remain; increase in next stitch; knit last stitch.

Row 31:

Knit 2 stitches; ***** purl 1 stitch, knit 1 stitch *****; repeat instructions between *****s across to last stitch; knit last stitch.

Row 32:

Knit each stitch.

Row 33:

Repeat Row 31.

Row 34:

Knit each stitch.

Row 35:

Repeat Row 31.

Row 36:

Repeat Row 30.

Rows 37 through 42:

Repeat Rows 25 through 30 once more.

You should now have 37 stitches.

Continue with "For All Sizes"" on page 74.

For sizes large and 1X only:

Rows 9 through 40:

Repeat Rows 1 through 8 four times more.

You should now have 41 stitches.

Continue with "For All Sizes" on page 74.

For size 2X only:

Rows 9 through 32:

Repeat Rows 1 through 8 three times more.

You should now have 39 stitches.

Row 33:

Work even in pattern as established.

Row 34:

Knit first stitch; increase in next stitch; knit to last 2 stitches; increase in next stitch; knit last stitch.

Rows 35 and 36:

Repeat Rows 33 and 34 once more.

You should now have 43 stitches. Continue with "For All Sizes" on page 74.

For size 3X only:

Rows 9 through 32:

Repeat Rows 1 through 8 three times more.

You should now have 39 stitches.

Row 33:

Work even in pattern as established.

Row 34:

Knit first stitch; increase in next stitch; knit to last 2 stitches; increase in next stitch; knit last stitch.

Rows 35 through 38:

Repeat Rows 33 and 34 twice more.

You should now have 45 stitches. Continue with "For All Sizes" below.

For All Sizes:

Row 1:

Work in pattern as established.

Row 2:

Knit each stitch.

Repeat Rows 1 and 2 until sleeve measures 16" (16", 16½", 16½", 17", 17") from cast-on edge, end by working a wrong side row **(Fig 13)**.

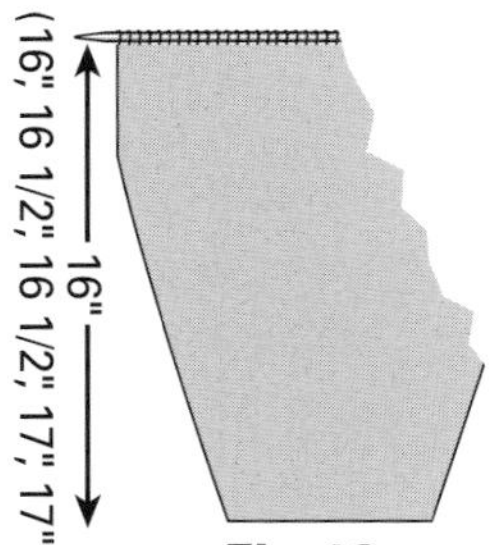

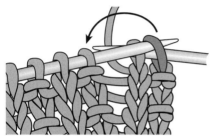

Fig 13

Armhole Shaping:
Armhole Shaping Row 1:

Bind off first 2 stitches as to knit **(Figs 14, 15 and 16)**; knit remaining stitches.

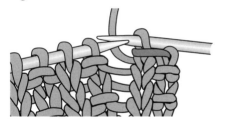

Fig 14

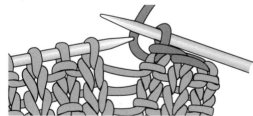

Fig 15

Fig 16

Armhole Shaping Row 2:

Bind off first 2 stitches as to purl (**Figs 17**, **18** and **19**); work in pattern as established across remaining stitches.

You should now have 33 (**33, 37, 37, 39, 41**) stitches.

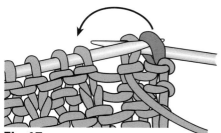

Fig 17

Fig 18

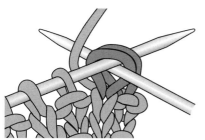

Fig 19

Cap Shaping:
Row 1:

Decrease by knitting first 2 stitches together (**Figs 20** and **21**); knit to last 2 stitches; decrease by knitting last 2 stitches together.

Row 2:

Work even in pattern as established.

Now you will work the next few rows differently depending on the size garment you are making.

Fig 20

For sizes small and medium only:

Next Row:

Knit each stitch.

Last Row:

Work even in pattern as established.

Loosely bind off all stitches as to knit.

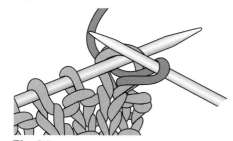

Fig 21

For sizes large and 1X only:

Repeat Rows 1 and 2 twice more; 31 stitches remain.

Next Row:

Knit each stitch.

Last Row:

Work even in pattern as established.

Loosely bind off all stitches as to knit.

For size 2X only:

Repeat Rows 1 and 2 three times more; 31 stitches remain.

Next Row:

Knit each stitch.

Last Row:

Work even in pattern as established.

Loosely bind off all stitches as to knit.

For size 3X only:

Repeat Rows 1 and 2 four times more; 31 stitches remain.

Next Row:

Knit each stitch.

Last Row:

Work even in pattern as established.

Loosely bind off all stitches as to knit.

Finishing

Note: Refer to Lesson 10 on page 21 for information on joining seams and weaving in ends. At this point you will need to decide which side you wish to have as the right side of your garment.

Place front and back flat as shown **(Fig 22)**. Weave shoulder seams together.

With pins, mark center of bound off edge of each sleeve. Place sleeves in armhole openings, matching center top of sleeve to shoulder seam, and bound off armhole stitches of sleeve to bound off armhole stitches of front and back **(Fig 23)**. Weave sleeves in place, easing to fit.

Match front and back sides and sleeve edges. Weave seams in continuous seam in direction as shown **(Fig 24)**.

Carefully weave in all loose yarn ends on wrong side of garment.

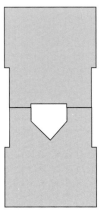

Fig 22

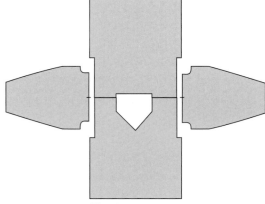

Fig 23

Fig 24

Challenge Sweater

Now that you're a knitter, here's a sweater that will be a challenge to knit, but well worth the effort.

Compare the color photos of this sweater and the Hug Me Sweater.

Can you tell that they are actually the same design? We've created this new look by combining different weights and types of yarn to add texture interest. The lighter weight yarns are worked with two strands held together; the heavier yarns, with just one strand. We used four different yarns, then we mixed six colors to create a really smashing garment.

Let's look at the yarns...

Lion Brand® Imagine — This is a worsted weight mohair/acrylic blend that is light and fluffy and comes in a variety of soft shades. We used 3 colors of Imagine in this sweater. We use it with two strands worked together.

Hint: Although Imagine is worked with strands from two different skeins held together, don't be tempted to wind the two skeins into one ball. Use the yarn just as it comes from the skeins. Be sure to keep your tension the same on both strands.

Lion Brand Chenille Sensations — Just like velvet, this wonderful yarn adds a luxurious sheen to your sweater. It comes in a range of solid colors and rich, deep jewel-tone combinations. We used one multi-color combination in this sweater. It is a worsted weight yarn, and we use it with two strands worked together.

Hint: Because Chenille Sensations yarn is slippery, it will be easier to work with if you will first wind each skein into a ball. Then work with one strand from each ball. Do not wind the two balls together. As you stitch, be sure that the tension is the same on both strands.

Lion Brand® Jiffy — A bulky weight yarn, this brushed acrylic looks just like mohair. Available in over 50 shades, heathers and multi-colors, we chose a deep multi-color shade. We use it in this sweater with one strand.

Lion Brand Homespun® — This bulky weight acrylic blend was chosen to add texture to our sweater. The yarn has a twist that sets it apart from the others. Available in solids and color blends, we chose one blended color which we use with one strand.

We know you'll have fun working with these exciting yarns. If you are unable to find these yarns at your favorite store, contact Lion Brand at 1-800-258-YARN.

The Challenge Sweater is shown in color photographs on the front cover and on page 25.

Sizing:

This sweater has an easy comfortable fit, with 4" to 8" allowed for ease.

Note: Pattern is written for size medium with changes for other sizes in parentheses.

All measurements are approximate.

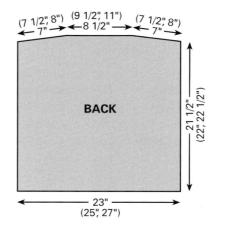

Size	Body Measurement at Bust	Finished Garment Measurement at Bust
Medium	34"-38"	46"
Large	40"-44"	50"
X-Large	46"-50"	54"

Materials:

Color A — Lion Brand® Imagine, Color 190, Mulberry, 2 skeins

Color B — Lion Brand Chenille Sensations, Color 409, Amsterdam, 2 skeins

Color C — Lion Brand® Imagine, Color 102, Aqua, 2 skeins

Color D — Lion Brand Jiffy®, Color 338, Manchester, 2 skeins

Color E — Lion Brand® Imagine, Color 191, Violet, 2 skeins

Color F — Lion Brand Homespun®, Color 303, Mission, 1 skein

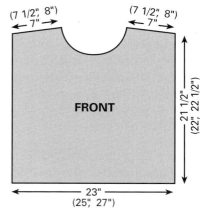

Equipment:

Size 13, 29" circular knitting needle, or size required for gauge

Size I aluminum crochet hook (for correcting mistakes and picking up stitches)

Two 6 1/4" long stitch holders

One 4 1/2" long stitch holder

Marker (for neck)

Size 13 steel tapestry sewing needle, or plastic yarn needle

Gauge:

In stockinette stitch (knit one row, purl one row) and with 2 strands of Imagine, 5 stitches = 2"

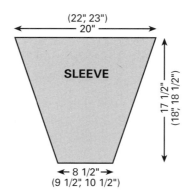

Making the Gauge Swatch:

To be sure the sweater will be the correct size, begin by making a sample swatch that will let you measure your gauge, as well as give you some practice working with two strands of yarn.

Take two balls of yarn and hold two strands together.

With both strands, cast on 20 stitches. Turn needle so that cast-on stitches are in left hand and last stitch cast-on is first stitch to be worked.

Row 1:
Being careful to use both strands at the same time, purl every stitch.

Row 2:
Being careful to use both strands at the same time, knit every stitch.

Repeat Rows 1 and 2 until you feel comfortable with the work, and your stitches are even. Work at least 18 rows. Loosely bind off all stitches. Then place the gauge swatch on a flat surface, and measure in center of swatch to see if the stitches are worked to gauge. There should be 5 stitches in every two inches. If you do not have 5 stitches in every two inches, see Lesson 8 on page 19.

When the gauge is just right, you're ready to start the sweater.

Color Pattern:

Row 1 (right side):
With 2 strands of Color B, knit each stitch.

Rows 2 through 4:
Knit each stitch. Cut Color B.

Row 5:
With 2 strands of Color C, knit each stitch.

Row 6:
Knit each stitch. Cut Color C.

Row 7:
With 1 strand of Color D, knit 2 stitches, slip 2 stitches as to purl (**Figs 1** and **2**); ***** carrying yarn loosely across slipped stitches (if carried yarn is pulled tightly it will pucker up the row), knit 2 stitches, slip 2 stitches as to purl *****; repeat instructions between *****s across row.

Row 8:
Purl each stitch, including the slipped stitches.

Row 9:
Knit each stitch.

Row 10:
Purl each stitch.

Rows 11 through 14:
Repeat Rows 9 and 10 twice. At end of Row 14, cut Color D.

Row 15:
With 2 strands of Color E, knit each stitch.

Rows 16 through 18:
Repeat Row 15. At end of Row 18, cut Color E.

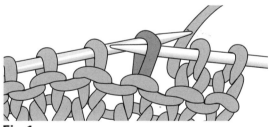

Fig 1

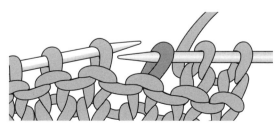

Fig 2

Row 19:
With 1 strand of Color F, * knit 2 stitches, slip 2 stitches as to purl *; repeat instructions between *s across row.

Row 20:
Purl each stitch, including the slipped stitches.

Row 21:
Knit each stitch.

Row 22:
Purl each stitch. Cut Color F.

Row 23:
With Color A, * knit 2 stitches, slip 2 stitches as to purl *; repeat instructions between *s across row.

Row 24:
Purl each stitch, including the slipped stitches.

Row 25:
Knit each stitch.

Row 26:
Purl each stitch.

Rows 27 and 28:
Repeat Rows 25 and 26. At end of Row 28, cut Color A.

Repeat Rows 1 through 28 for Color Pattern.

Sweater Instructions

Note: Pattern is written for size medium with changes for other sizes in parentheses.

Back
With 2 strands of Color A held together, cast on 58 (62, 68) stitches. Turn needle so that cast-on stitches are in left hand and last stitch cast-on is first stitch to be worked.

Row 1 (right side of garment):
Knit each stitch.

Row 2:
Purl each stitch.

For size medium only:

Repeat Rows 1 and 2 once more. At end of last row, cut Color A.

Continue with "Body" on page 81.

For size large only:

Repeat Rows 1 and 2 twice more. At end of last row, cut Color A.

Continue with "Body" on page 81.

For size X-large only:

Repeat Rows 1 and 2 three times more. At end of last row, cut Color A.

Continue with "Body" on page 81.

Body:

Now begin to work in Color Pattern. Work 2 complete Color Pattern repeats. Then work Rows 1 through 24 of Color Pattern. This is the length the sweater will be to the shoulders.

Shoulder Shaping:

Now we'll shape the shoulders by binding off several stitches at the beginning of each of the next four rows. Continuing in Color Pattern:

Shoulder Row 1:

With 2 strands of Color A, loosely bind off the first 9 (9, 10) stitches as to knit; then knit the remaining stitches.

Shoulder Row 2:

Loosely bind off the first 9 (9, 10) stitches as to purl; then purl the remaining stitches.

You should now have 40 (44, 48) stitches.

Shoulder Row 3:

Loosely bind off the first 9 (10, 10) stitches as to knit; then knit the remaining stitches.

Shoulder Row 4:

Loosely bind off the first 9 (10, 10) stitches as to purl; then purl the remaining stitches.

You should now have 22 (24, 28) stitches.

These stitches will be used later to form the back of the neck. We're not going to bind off these stitches, instead we are going to set them safely aside. So take the 6 1/4" stitch holder, and slip the remaining stitches on it. Cut yarn, leaving a 6" yarn end and set piece aside.

Front

With 2 strands of Color A held together, cast on 58 (62, 68) stitches.

Row 1 (right side of garment):

Knit each stitch.

Row 2:

Purl each stitch.

For size medium only:

Repeat Rows 1 and 2 once more. At end of last row, cut Color A.

Continue with "Body" on page 82.

For size large only:

Repeat Rows 1 and 2 twice more. At end of last row, cut Color A.

Continue with "Body" on page 82.

For size X-large only:

Repeat Rows 1 and 2 three times more. At end of last row, cut Color A.

Continue with "Body" on page 82.

Body:

Now begin to work in Color Pattern. Work 2 complete Color Pattern repeats. Then work Rows 1 through 16 of Color Pattern. This is the length the sweater will be to the front neckline.

Note: We worked this piece about 2" shorter than the back to allow for the front neckline, which is lower than the back neckline. On the next row you will place the stitches reserved for the neck onto a stitch holder, and the stitches for the Right Shoulder on another stitch holder. The remaining stitches are for the Left Shoulder.

Left Neckline Row 1 (right side of garment):
Working Row 17 of Color Pattern, knit the first 26 (27, 29) stitches for Left Shoulder; slip the next 6 (8, 10) stitches onto the 4¹/₂" stitch holder for the front neck; slip the remaining 26 (27, 29) stitches to the second 6¹/₄" stitch holder for the Right Shoulder.

Left Neckline Row 2:
Working Row 18 of Color Pattern, bind off the first 4 stitches as to knit; knit remaining stitches.

Left Neckline Row 3:
Work Row 19 of Color Pattern.

Left Neckline Row 4:
Working Row 20 of Color Pattern, bind off the first 4 (4, 5) stitches as to purl; purl remaining stitches.

You should now have 18 (19, 20) stitches.

Now repeat Rows 21 through 24 of Color Pattern.

Left Shoulder Shaping:
Row 1:
Working Row 25 of Color Pattern, bind off first 9 (9, 10) stitches as to knit; knit remaining stitches.

Row 2:
Work Row 26 of Color Pattern.

Loosely bind off all stitches as to knit.

Cut yarn, leaving a 6" yarn end.

Right Neckline:
Slip 26 (27, 29) shoulder stitches from stitch holder to free end of needle; join Color E in first stitch at neck edge on right side of Right Shoulder.

Right Neckline Row 1 (right side of garment):
Working Row 17 of Color Pattern, bind off first 4 (4, 5) stitches as to knit; knit remaining stitches.

Right Neckline Row 2:
Work Row 18 of Color Pattern.

Right Neckline Row 3:
Working Row 19 of Color Pattern, bind off first 4 (4, 5) stitches as to knit; work remaining stitches in Color Pattern.

Right Neckline Row 4:
Work Row 20 of Color Pattern.

You should now have 18 (19, 20) stitches.

Now repeat Rows 21 through 24 of Color Pattern.

Right Shoulder Shaping:
Row 1:
Work Row 25 of Color Pattern.
Row 2:
Working Row 26 of Color Pattern, bind off first 9 (9, 10) stitches as to purl; purl remaining stitches.
Row 3:
Work Row 27 of Color Pattern.

Loosely bind off all stitches as to purl.

Cut yarn, leaving a 6" yarn end and set piece aside.

Sleeve (make 2)

With two strands of Color A, cast on 22 (24, 26) stitches.
Row 1 (right side of garment):
Knit each stitch.
Row 2:
Purl each stitch.
Row 3:
Knit first stitch, increase by knitting in front and back of next stitch; knit across to last 2 stitches; increase by knitting in front and back of next stitch; knit last stitch.

You should now have 24 (26, 28) stitches.
Row 4:
Purl each stitch.
Row 5:
Knit each stitch.
Row 6:
Purl each stitch. Cut Color A.

Begin to work in Color Pattern, increasing in second stitch and next to last stitch of Row 1. Then increase in second stitch and next to last stitch of every fourth row.

Work 2 complete Color Pattern repeats.

Repeat Row 1 of Color Pattern, increasing in second and next to last stitch of row.

You should now have 50 (56, 58) stitches.

Work even in Color Pattern to Row 10 (10, 12).

Loosely bind off all remaining stitches as to purl.

Collar

Before knitting the collar, it is necessary to sew the shoulder seams. Place back and front flat with right sides facing you. Referring to Lesson 10 on page 21, weave shoulder seams.

Now you will work the collar in one piece.

You begin by "picking up" stitches along the shaped front neck edges, and working the stitches from the holders.

Hold sweater with right side facing you and neckline at top.

Pick up 12 (14, 14) stitches down left side of neck edge; sl next 6 (8, 10) stitches from front holder to free end of needle; knit these stitches; pick up 12 (14, 14) stitches up right side of neck edge; slip the 22 (24, 28) stitches from stitch holder to free end of needle; knit these stitches.

You should now have 52 (60, 66) stitches.

Note: Now it is necessary to place a marker (either a purchased plastic one or a loop of yarn) on the needle before knitting the first stitch to mark the beginning of the round.

The collar is made in one piece by working in rounds. (This means after working all stitches, do not turn needle; slip the marker and continue working in same direction.) All rounds are knitted.

You will begin the first round by working in the first stitch you picked up along the left-hand side of neck edge.

Round 1:
Knit each stitch.

Rounds 2 through 11:
Repeat Round 1.

Loosely bind off all stitches as to knit.

Collar will roll naturally to right side of sweater.

Finishing

Note: Refer to Lesson 10 on page 21 for information on joining seams and weaving in ends.

Open joined piece out on a flat surface. Measure down 10" (11", 11½") from shoulder seam on both sides of front and back and mark with pins; mark center of bound off edge of each sleeve **(Fig 3)**.

Match marked centers of sleeves to shoulder seam and edge of sleeves to marked points on front and back of sweater. Weave each sleeve in place.

Place front and back with side seams and sleeve edges together. Weave side and sleeve seams in continuous seam in direction as shown **(Fig 4)**.

Carefully weave in all loose yarn ends on wrong side of garment.

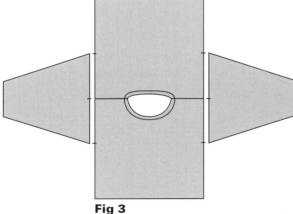

Fig 3

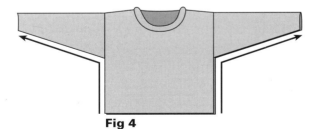

Fig 4